I0070020

PERFECT APPROACH

A 9-HOLE COURSE
TO FINANCIAL SUCCESS BEYOND THE 9 TO 5

KYLE RUDDUCK, CFA, CFP®

Published by Kyle Rudduck

Copyright © Kyle Rudduck, 2018

I look forward to following *your* Perfect Approach to living life! So that I can follow your success, please use the hashtag #PerfectApproach on social media so that we can build a community of like-minded birdie-chasers!

For my dad who taught me the game, my mom who sacrificed her time to allow me to grow with the game, and my wife who allows me to continue to enjoy the game.

For Coach Mudd who showed me the true meaning of courage and taught me how much fun the game of golf can be.

Thank you!

Why Write a Book About Golf and Finance?

Golf is an amazing game. My dad introduced me to it when I was 4 years old and, as he told me then, "It's a game you can play for the rest of your life, but you'll never fully master." Almost nothing else I've experienced in life has had quite the same ability to challenge, humble, and drive internal, emotional swings that change more quickly than those of a toddler at an amusement park. *Almost* nothing, that is, aside from managing personal finances.

While golf was my first passion in life, as I grew older and realized that this 10-plus handicapper didn't have much of a shot at making it on the pro tour, I came to follow my second passion: helping people avoid costly mistakes in managing their own finances. As a CFA charterholder and Certified Financial Planner®, I've dedicated my professional life to building the expertise necessary to assist hundreds of clients along their journeys of achieving financial success and pursuing passions away from their 9 to 5 jobs. I've come to understand the financial questions that are most commonly on the minds of individuals and learned solutions to help them most efficiently solve their problems. And that is why I wanted to write this book.

But why golf? Countless sources indicate that we, as Americans, are terrible at managing our personal finances and (perhaps related to that) susceptible to falling for the latest investment fads or get-rich-quick schemes. (Bitcoin or Bernie Madoff, anyone?) However, I feel strongly that our shortsightedness is not a function of willfully neglecting our future, but rather a byproduct of what psychologist Barry Schwartz refers to as *the paradox of choice*. That is, we're so overwhelmed by the sheer number of options available to us (and so much conflicting advice) that we justify to ourselves that by taking no action, we at least won't make the wrong decision.

But it doesn't need to be that complicated.

It all comes down to three concepts: risk vs. return, a focus on controlling only the variables you can, and avoiding mental mistakes. And all three concepts are as relevant to your round of golf as they are in managing your personal finances. By leveraging analogies using the game of golf, my goal for this book is to break down complex financial concepts into terms that can be easily understood and applied to immediately begin improving your finances.

But why 9 holes? An 18-hole round can be intimidating for a beginning golfer—and even experienced ones who are in the middle of a bad round. Playing 18 holes can also be quite the time commitment. By the time you hop in the car, drive to the course, hit a few range balls, and finish your round, 6 or 7 hours could have easily passed by. The result is that most of us don't play as much as we'd like.

But a quick 9? You can squeeze 9 holes in on a Wednesday evening after wrapping up a full day at the office. You can take your young daughter or son out to enjoy a quick 9 together on the course and still make it home in time for dinner. Playing 9 holes is a much less daunting task than 18 and it doesn't monopolize an entire day. As a result, the game can become much more enjoyable and more likely to be engaged.

Such is the goal for this book. I've used the game of golf to draw analogies that will simplify what may otherwise seem like intimidating financial concepts and strategies. By arming yourself with a better understanding of the financial industry and the key factors most likely to impact you, the end result will be an improvement in your finances and an enjoyment of the process.

Regardless of whether you're a scratch golfer or 36-handicapper, I hope the material in the pages to come will become your go-to guide. Think of it as a yardage book that you can use to help navigate the course of your financial life.

-Kyle Rudduck
September, 2018

COURSE MAP

Introduction

"Keep shooting pars, a**hole," Roy "Tin Cup" McAvoy chirps at his opponent, Dave Sims.

"I'll take 18 of them, all day long," Sims replies.

"Do it and I'll own you!" responds McAvoy.

In what goes down as one of the greatest golf movies of all time, *Tin Cup*, the above exchange between Roy McAvoy and his rival, Dave Sims, is one of my favorite scenes from the entire film. Roy, the brash, fun-loving, driving range pro (played by Kevin Costner at his finest) gets a crack at playing in the U.S. Open, razzing his always-by-the-book opponent that simply making pars will not be good enough to best him. However, anyone who has seen the film knows how it ends.

In golf, mental mistakes and unnecessary risk taking will eventually ruin you. We elect to use the driver and go for the green, when the smart play would be laying up into position with a 7-iron. The result often leaves us longing for par as we stand over a 3-foot putt for double bogey.

All too frequently, this same longing will also envelop our financial lives when a sound plan is suddenly derailed. Perhaps it was getting caught up in a fad. Or perhaps it was allowing emotion to get

1

the better of our rational selves in the midst of a panicked market. No matter the cause, the result is watching what was otherwise a steady round become a scramble to recover and salvage whatever's left.

Bobby Jones once referred to golf as a game that is played on a five-inch course—the space between your ears. Warren Buffett described temperament as being the most important trait of an investor, not intellect. While Buffett and Jones took entirely different paths in their careers and professional lives, both understood and highlighted the critical role that our minds play in determining success or failure in both the game of golf and our finances.

In the pages to come, lessons from the game of golf will be used to improve our mental awareness of personal finance and to teach various financial strategies that will set you up for success. Along the way, I will dispel some of the myths, highlight many of the opportunities, and challenge some common "rules of thumb" that will likely be encountered along your journey—starting from the first tee shot all the way through your final putt.

I hope you enjoy the read and start finding many more financial fairways and greens as a result!

Hole #1: The First Tee Shot

"The most important shot in golf is the next one."–
Ben Hogan

Have you ever stood on the first tee without having had time to warm up? Do you recall the feeling in your stomach as you stood over the ball, having absolutely no idea where the first swing of the day may cause the ball to go? I know I have—more than once! And I also know the outcomes of that first shot can be mixed. I've striped drives down the middle of the fairway and snap-hooked a few directly out of bounds. But the great thing about the first tee shot is, no matter the outcome, there is an entire round that remains to be played. Hit a great first shot? Fantastic. Hit a terrible first shot? There's plenty of time to recover.

This holds just as true with investing. It's not about how your first shot turns out; you're just getting started. Once you get off the first tee, whether with a driver or an iron, the rest of the round remains to be played. And the earlier you can do it, the sooner your swing can find its groove.

As you set out on your path to financial freedom, the biggest asset on your side is the power of time and compounding. Compounding interest on top of interest allows you to begin setting aside small pieces of your income early on, while ending your career with a multimillion-dollar nest egg. And the earlier you start, the easier it is to reach your financial goals with the least amount of impact on your day to day.

To illustrate, consider the following example of two savers, Jordan and Phil, each beginning their financial journey:

	Jordan	Phil
Amount Saved per Year	$5,000	$10,000
Age Started	20	35
Age Stopped	35	60
Total Years Spent Saving	15	25
Total Amount Saved	$5,000×15=$75,000	$10,000×25=$250,000
Age at Retirement	60	60
Account Value at Retirement	$930,000	$731,000

Jordan gets an early start on his saving by putting away $5,000 a year when he is just 20 years old. Upon reaching his 35th birthday, however, he decides he no longer wants to save at all. Over the course of 15 years, Jordan has saved a total of $75,000. He plans to retire at age 60.

Phil gets a late start and doesn't begin saving until he is 35 years old. But he is able to put away $10,000 a year until he retires at age 60. Over 25 years, Phil saves a combined total of $250,000.

Although Phil saved more than 3 times as much as Jordan, the scorecard tells the tale: Due to the power of compounding, the balance of Jordan's $930,000 account at age 60 is nearly $200,000 more than Phil's $731,000 balance[i].

Finally, just for fun, let's assume that instead of stopping his savings contributions at age 35, Jordan continued to save each year until he retired at age 60. Simply by continuing to contribute the same amount—just $5,000 per year—his account balance at age 60 would have grown to $1.3 million. This, despite still contributing a total of $200,000, $50,000 less than Phil did over his career!

The point is, no matter where you are on your journey towards your financial goals, starting now is better than starting later. The power of time and compounding are on the same side, and the longer you have them working for you, the more powerful the effects can become.

Maybe you've heard similar examples before. You know all of this already. So why, then, is it still such a struggle to get started? And more importantly, how can it be fixed?

Reason #1: Willful neglect

In a joint study conducted by the University of Michigan Retirement Research Center and the Social Security Administration, researchers polled a number of different workers about their employer-sponsored retirement plans (e.g., 401(k) accounts)[ii]. Their goal was to assess how well workers understood their plans and measure their level of participation. The findings of the study were incredible. For instance, while the median worker *reported* contributing $2,328 to his or her retirement plan, the numbers showed that those same workers were actually deferring only $1,300. In other words, the typical retiree was contributing nearly 45% *less* than what they thought they were! Imagine the surprise if this were to continue each of their working years. Upon reaching retirement and looking at their accounts, it would surely be a shock to find that their budgets needed to be slashed by 45% (or more) as a result of the misalignment of their presumptions with reality.

We all tend to get caught up in the day-to-day hustle of life. There is a mortgage to pay, food to buy, and our children's sports seasons to tend to. As a result of everything going on in the here and now, it's easy to neglect our future selves, instead promising that "we'll get started next month" or "start fresh with the new year." The challenge is, expenses don't stop. And as pay raises are earned, the expenses seem to magically increase as well. Before you know it, next month has turned into next year and next year has morphed into 5 years down the road. But knowing the advantages starting earlier can provide, how can you most effectively change your behavior to increase the odds of taking action?

Visualization and discipline.

In a separate study conducted at the University of Stanford's Virtual Human Interaction Lab[iii], researchers used artificial intelligence to create lifelike avatars of the participants. These computer-generated images showed the study's participants as aged, future versions of their current selves. The outcome of this study was that individuals who were shown such images, as compared to those that were shown versions of themselves at their current age, contributed significantly more to their hypothetical savings accounts.

The findings of the study demonstrated that by visualizing ourselves at a later point in life, we're able to increase empathy levels for our future selves. The result is that saving is no longer perceived as throwing money at an arbitrary bucket, but rather a fruitful exercise with a meaningful benefit. What if instead of asking yourself what you may be missing out on by not making a purchase today, you instead visualized yourself turning off your alarm clock at 7 on the morning of your 75th birthday? Or instead of hitting the links on a beautiful summer morning with your friends, you're headed into the office to earn the paycheck needed to pay the mortgage. Ouch!

The point is, saving does not have to be painful, but you need to have a reason for doing it. Absent an objective or your "Why," as author Simon Sinek would say, success is difficult to visualize and saving for the future will seem much more arbitrary.

Prevent yourself from falling into the trap of overspending today and sacrificing your tomorrow by hacking your mind to visualize your older, future version. Are you picturing yourself as being early to the practice range on Wednesday morning or as the first one in the office, brewing a pot of coffee for your co-workers?

Reason #2: I'm waiting for the market to come down—it's too high right now!

What if I told you there's an investment I could offer you that has increased by more than 10% *each year* over each of the past 30 years? In addition, this investment would have outperformed all of your friends' investments by more than 6% in each of those years[iv]? Sounds too good to be true, right? Actually, the investment I'm referring to is nothing other than buying and holding the S&P 500. And the weak returns your friends generated? They're the result of falling into the trap of believing they've discovered a strategy to "time the market." That is, they've decided that, rather than simply stay invested, they have insight that will allow them to know when to jump in and when to jump out.

"I'm going to wait for the market to pull back a little...or calm down...or get through this election...or see what the next jobs report says..." I hear those types of comments all the time. But the reality is, the market cannot be timed. And as study after study continues to indicate, individuals that try to do it will lose—oftentimes significantly. The fortunate thing though, is that you don't have to be perfect to be successful. Far from it, actually.

In a study completed by the Schwab Center for Financial Research[v], researchers examined the outcomes of 5 different hypothetical investors. Each investor had $2,000 to invest per year for 20 consecutive years. However, each investor chose a different strategy to determine how/when to put their cash to work, as follows:

1. Perfect Phil: Phil chose exactly the market bottom in each year to put his $2,000 to

work. That is, he perfectly chose the market bottom of each year and invested his $2,000 on that day.

2. Immediate Ian: Ian chose simply to invest his $2,000 at the earliest possible opportunity, on the first investment day of each year.

3. Dollar Cost Dustin: Dustin elects to invest 1/12 of his $2,000 ($167/month) into the market over each month of the year.

4. Accidental Arnold: Arnold is the exact, unlucky opposite of Phil. Rather than pick the best day to invest each year, Arnold chooses the absolute worst day to invest, putting his $2,000 to work at each year's market high point.

5. Cash Is King Charlie: Charlie takes his $2,000 and elects not to invest at all. That is, rather than put his money into the market, Charlie takes the $2,000 each year and puts it into a savings account.

At the end of the 20-year period, the figure below details the cumulative value of each investor's portfolio:

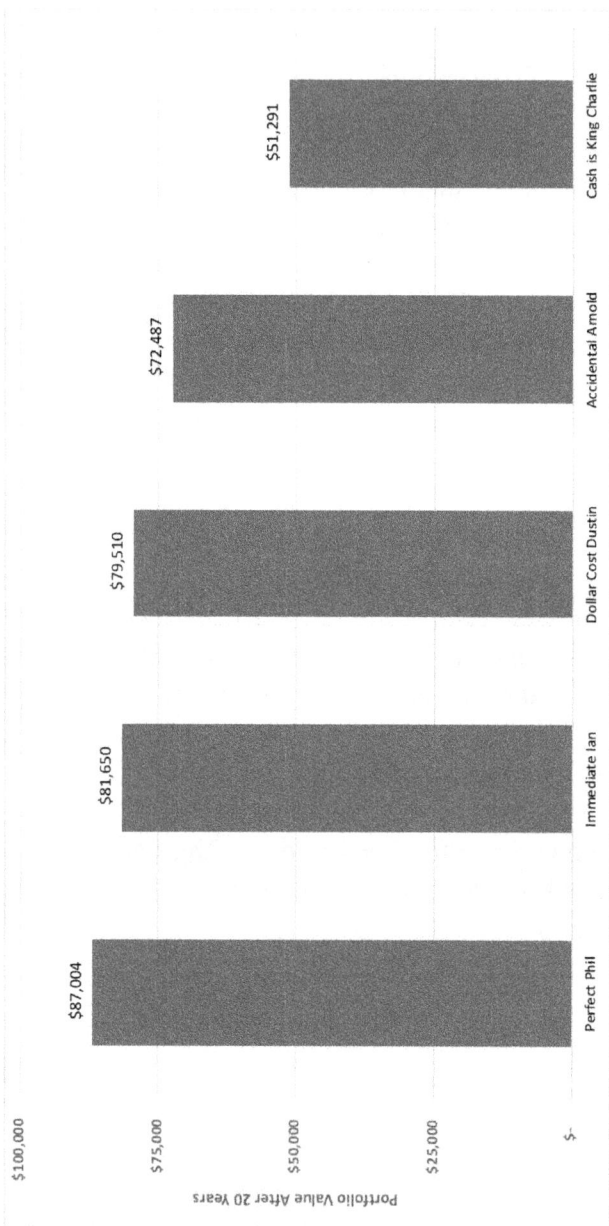

Portfolio Value After 20 Years

Perfect Phil	$87,004
Immediate Ian	$81,650
Dollar Cost Dustin	$79,510
Accidental Arnold	$72,487
Cash is King Charlie	$51,291

Not surprisingly, Perfect Phil, the investor who timed the market "perfectly" for 20 years straight, wound up accumulating the largest account balance at the end of the period. But what may surprise you is that Phil's reward for being perfect (an impossible feat in reality) was a mere 6.5% edge over Immediate Ian, who simply invested his cash at the earliest possible opportunity.

Perhaps what is most remarkable about this study's findings, however, is that the biggest loser was not the investor who timed the market perfectly wrong. In fact, while Accidental Arnold did everything wrong from a timing perspective, he still bested Cash is King Charlie by more than 41%! I'll say again: Over the course of 20 years, Accidental Arnold chose the worst possible day each year to invest his money into the market and still ended up with a portfolio that was 41% larger than his counterpart who chose to never invest at all. Based on data in the above chart, perhaps the biggest risk to our investment portfolios is not the market itself but rather our own fear and inertia to take action.

When choosing to invest money, it is important to remember the 3 things that can happen after electing to put cash to work:

1. The market goes up and you're better off.

2. The market stays at its current level but pays a dividend that is greater than the interest currently being earned in a savings account.
3. The market temporarily declines and provides a further buying opportunity. (We'll discuss more about this on Hole #7.)

Any of the above 3 scenarios can be a positive if you're prepared. And over extended periods of time, the research suggests that any of those 3 options will fare better than sitting in cash on the sidelines. So, what are you waiting for? It's time to get in the game!

To make things easier, consider the following tips for getting started:

1. **Save automatically:** Just as your golf score would improve if every putt were a gimmie, electing to make savings happen automatically can significantly improve your financial positioning. Pay yourself first by taking advantage of recurring monthly contributions from spending to savings accounts or, better yet, have amounts deducted directly from your paycheck and deferred automatically to your savings account. By making savings automatic, you avoid having to remember to do it each month and because money is going directly

into savings, there is less temptation to spend it.

2. **Take full advantage of raises:** Just received notice that you've earned an increase in your salary next year or are due a bonus? Congratulations! Now, increase the percentage of your income that you contribute to your savings account. If you do it immediately, this is a rare instance when you can have your cake and eat it, too! Deferring a percentage of the increase obviously increases your savings, but it also allows your current self to enjoy part of the raise as well. By causing the increase to happen immediately, you also prevent yourself from succumbing to so-called lifestyle creep—increasing your lifestyle spending by an amount equal to or greater than the pay raise you just earned. Lifestyle creep is a monster to be avoided at all costs for two main reasons. First, the more expensive lifestyle is one that you'll be tempted to maintain into the future (i.e., higher spending in retirement); second, the higher spending reduces your ability to fund that lifestyle due to having less available to save today.

3. **Think of purchases in terms of their opportunity costs:** Each dollar spent is a dollar that is not invested. Investments, by definition, are assets that we expect to

appreciate in value over time and provide benefit to us for an indefinite period into the future. For each dollar that is spent frivolously, there is one dollar that is no longer available to work for your future self. Remember that each time you're tempted to purchase a new golf glove. Think maybe you could get it to last one more round?

Hole #2: Get the Mind Right

"Success in golf depends less on strength of body than upon strength of mind."—Arnold Palmer

Golf is a funny game. One day you feel as though you have everything figured out and the next day you walk off the course having played so poorly you swear off ever picking up another club. Personally, I can recall a stint last summer when I developed a case of the snap hooks off the tee (simply *infuriating,* to say the least) and seriously considered taking the remainder of the season off. Instead, I decided to work through it. Range time, course time, swings in the garage, swings in the backyard—anywhere with enough space to swing a club, I was taking advantage. Anything to try and get rid of my swing funk.

By simply continuing to swing the club, eventually I started to see a couple of shots improve. As the outcome of those shots began to improve, so did my confidence. And as my confidence started to come back, even more shots improved until, just as quickly as I'd lost my swing, it was found again. By the end of that summer, my confidence was at an all-time high and I even challenged myself to compete in the club championship at my local golf course. The emotional rollercoaster of that summer took me from nearly swearing off the game, to ultimately winning the local club championship—all without any noticeable changes aside from my mental attitude. Throughout the process, I re-learned just how much of a mental sport the game of golf truly is.

So often, the fiercest competitor on the course is none other than the space between our own two ears.

In much the same way, there are mental obstacles that will likely plague you along your journey of planning your financial life. However, by better understanding some of the common culprits and increasing your awareness of the hazards they may lead you into, steps can be taken to *proactively* correct your path and avoid incurring penalty shots unnecessarily.

Mental Bunker #1: The Gambler
My dad always quoted the familiar adage "Drive for show, putt for dough," and I remind myself of this constantly when it comes to planning. I have a favorite hole at my home course. It's a par 4 that doesn't play particularly long—often just about 300 yards—but it has a peninsula green flanked on three sides by water. No matter the round I have going, every time I step on to the tee box at #14, I always find myself tempted to go for it. The number of times I've successfully driven the green pales in comparison to the number of golf balls I've donated

to the pond. Yet the feeling of connecting the club purely with the ball and racing up to see it sitting directly in the green's center is enough to tempt me every time.

Investors often find themselves facing a similar challenge: wanting to gamble on picking the next "hot" stock. We're enamored with the possibility that one correct pick could catapult us towards financial independence and often the mere idea of this possibility clouds better judgment. We ignore how, if picked incorrectly, the stock could splash into the pond and jeopardize an otherwise great plan.

The financial media loves to capitalize on our desire to gamble and does so with the likes of all sorts of publications and talk shows. They're constantly promising how they're going to provide us the information to discover the next Amazon or Apple. The challenge is, they are in the entertainment business, not the advisory business and without the hype, they would all soon be out of jobs.

There is a reason the majority of financial news sites' homepages, and even our investment accounts, more closely resemble the sights and sounds of a Las Vegas casino than a calm day at the golf course. They are designed to encourage activity and action that generate revenue for the hosts. However, if there is one thing we can all agree on, it's that the city of Las Vegas was not built by the gamblers who won. The house always has the edge.

Whether you buy or sell, speculate or invest, many financial firms make money based on activity and subscriptions and are therefore incentivized to keep you chasing the next hot investment. And while electing to follow their lead may be a good retirement strategy for them, right now we're focusing on your plan. We know penalty shots can quickly derail a great round of golf and we must remember that losses can quickly accumulate to derail a great financial plan. Accordingly, prudent investors must force themselves to stay focused on strategies that are statistically shown to put the odds in their favor, in turn, driving the most value over the course of a long-term plan.

How to beat the gambler:
Have a plan! As discussed in chapter 1, visualizing the future can go a long way in helping improve upon savings strategy. It can also work to keep you focused on your own game while all the other investors get caught up in events like the tech market bubble of the early 2000s or the Great Recession of 2008–2009. By having a plan and understanding what is required of you and your portfolio to meet your goals, you're less likely to be duped into pursuing a strategy that could lead to you being disadvantaged—or outright taken advantage of!

If you are one of those personality types that simply prefers to grip and rip with every shot, having a plan can satisfy your appetite for risk but in a more controlled manner. Specifically, if you've developed a plan that has been designed to show how much is required to achieve retirement success, a Go for the Green account can be set up on the side with *excess* savings once you're trending on the appropriate path. The total value of this account should be an amount that would not be catastrophic if lost entirely. That is, even if the value of the investments within your Go for the Green account went to $0, the rest of your round would remain secure.

Mental Bunker #2: Confirmation Bias

Just a couple of summers ago, I was on the hunt for a new driver. The driver that I had at the time was nearly 5 years old and I was certain that having a new one would better my game. I ventured over to a local golf store that offered fittings and had computer software that would analyze my swing, thus matching me with the perfect new club. I even took my old driver with me for comparison's sake.

As the process began, I first took a couple of swings with my current driver to get a baseline reading of my stats. From there, I began trying drivers from different companies, with different shaft combinations and lie angles to determine my ideal club and setup. Though I could see the results on the machine were not reading much different from new driver to old, I was convinced that the club just "felt" better and would soon be adding 25 yards to my average tee shot. Convinced of what I needed before I even entered the store, obviously, I had to buy it.

After playing a couple of rounds with the new stick, I knew that I wasn't getting the results I wanted. In hindsight, I realize that I tended to remember only the best tee shots of each round in an attempt to convince myself that I was in a better position with the new club and, most importantly, that I'd made the correct decision to purchase it in the first place.

One day, after having owned the club for a couple of months, I headed out to the range to see if I could get it dialed in just right. Much to my surprise, I was dead wrong. Not only was I not getting the distance to which I was accustomed, but I was also beginning to lose shots left and right. Feeling completely discouraged, I started to walk off the range. As I made the walk back towards the parking lot, I happened to look down and notice my old driver staring back at me from the golf bag. I paused for a minute and then took the club out of the bag. My first shot was a rocket. The second one went even farther than the first, and the third sealed the deal. I immediately went back to the store and traded in the new driver for a couple dozen golf balls and a new glove and continue to play with my time-tested model to this day. (Side lesson learned: The trade-in programs at golf stores make new car mark-ups seem like the deal of the century!)

The example above highlights a mental trap that's commonly incurred in the investing world as well. Referred to as confirmation bias, it's a tendency to consider only the information that will confirm the beliefs we already have, as opposed to being open to new information that may cause a change in mindset (or, gasp, force us to admit we were wrong). I convinced myself that I needed a new driver before stepping foot into the golf store and as a result, I ignored the information from the club fitting and also the results I was seeing on the course.

Confirmation bias can happen anywhere, but politics and investing are two areas in which we tend to be particularly susceptible. We have beliefs that we feel *must* absolutely be true. Then we spend the majority of our time reading like-minded authors, watching like-minded television shows, and scanning like-minded websites that will reinforce those beliefs. But we must be aware of this bias and its potential to impact our investment decision-making. As you look to build and maintain your retirement plans and investment portfolios, ensure you haven't made up your mind on what's appropriate before you've assessed what you need.

How to outthink confirmation bias:
Ask more questions!

Ask questions not only of yourself but also of individuals whose views are different from your own. Questions like:
"What if I am wrong?"
"What could I stand to lose if I'm wrong?"
"What does the person across the table see that causes them to feel so differently about this issue than me?"

Warren Buffett, arguably the greatest investor of all time, attributes much of his success to his willingness to listen to points counter to his own and not let his emotions and personal biases interfere with logic.

Consider researching opinions alternative to your own with an open mind and a commitment to letting logic prevail. Pose questions to those you know and respect, especially those with expertise in the areas critical to where your decision is being made. Once the question is asked, listen. Do not filter a response, keeping only the nuggets that agree with your initial thought. Take in everything, particularly potential blind spots that could present major risks down the road.

Mental Bunker #3: Loss Aversion

In *Thinking Fast and Slow*, Nobel Prize-winning author and psychologist Daniel Kahneman outlines a number of behavioral studies about how our minds work and process thoughts. At one point, Kahneman describes a study in which over 2.5 million putts were analyzed to determine if a golfer's concentration levels are different when putting for par vs. putting for birdie. The results? Regardless of distance and level of difficulty, a golfer is 3.6% more likely to sink a putt for par than a similar one for birdie!

Part of the logic underlying this phenomenon is a behavioral bias known as loss aversion: We tend to incur more pain from losses than pleasure from gains. In the golf world, Kahneman's study demonstrated that, while it may be nice to score a birdie and celebrate for a moment, we loathe the pain associated with making a bogey—pain that can linger with us for a number of holes. As a result, our focus tends to improve on putts for par and more of them are holed.

In the investment world, loss aversion can lead us to avoid the stock market altogether, or worse, sell stocks in a panic (at exactly the wrong time) only because the thought of an investment declining further can't be stomached. Awareness of loss aversion is a powerful tool, however, as it improves the ability to recognize the driving force behind a decision. Are you making a rational choice based on research or a change in financial circumstances? Are you making an impulse decision in an attempt to help avoid feelings of pain or regret? Understanding the thought process that is driving decision-making at any given time will assist tremendously in preventing emotion from getting the better of logic.

Don't lose to loss aversion:
When is the best time to buy new golf balls? In the middle of peak season or in the middle of winter when the discount sales are in full swing? Obviously, the best time to buy is when the product is on sale. 10% off? Great! 25% off? Fantastic! 50% off? Back the truck up, I'm buying whatever is left. The answer seems so clear when referencing golf balls or golf clubs, so there's no reason it should become confusing when referencing investments instead. Purchasing a good investment that is on sale at 25% off is better than paying full price in peak season.

In the post-World War II era (December 1945–present), the S&P 500 has experienced several dozen price drops of more than 10%[vi]:

% Decline	# of Occurrences
10% – 19.9% ("Correction")	34
>20% ("Bear Market")	22
Total Corrections & Bear Markets	*56*

In the previous 73 years highlighted in the preceding chart, the market has gone on sale by experiencing either a correction or bear market roughly three out of every four years, on average. While merely gaining the understanding that volatility is a natural part of the market can add significant value alone, one of the key observations to make from the above data is how few corrections ultimately become bear markets: just 39%! The majority of the time, rather than looking to jump out of our investments upon experiencing a loss for fear of seeing further decline, history would suggest this is actually the time we should be taking advantage of the market's sale by purchasing more.

One of my all-time favorite quotes from Warren Buffett is: "Be fearful when others are greedy and be greedy when others are fearful." By preparing for the inevitable market correction or crash, you can put yourself in a position to capitalize on the opportunity when it presents (for more detail on how to capitalize on market volatility, see Hole #7).

Mental Bunker #4: Representativeness
Have you ever seen the investment disclaimer that reads "Past performance is not indicative of future results"? Do you ever wonder why that language is required compliance disclosure to investors?

A recent issue of *Golf Digest* contained a story titled "Our Prediction on Tiger Surpassing Jack's Record Didn't Quite Work Out." The piece outlined a very detailed timeline that originated in 2008—Tiger in his prime—which sought to predict when and where Tiger Woods would break Jack Nicklaus's record of major championship victories. Fast forwarding from that moment in time (and a 9-iron through the rear window of his Escalade later), it's now debatable if he will ever win another at all.

In 2008, Tiger stood alone at the summit of the golfing world and was the odds-on favorite to win any tournament he played in. It was only natural to suspect that his success would continue. Until, well, it didn't.

Many investors often make a very similar mistake when it comes to investment selection. It's easy to fall into the trap of thinking that because a stock or fund has performed well recently, it will continue to do so indefinitely.

You may have experienced this, for example, during the exercise of picking mutual funds to invest in within your 401(k). Instead of doing research, did you look at the performance history of particular funds and select those with the best track record? If so, you are certainly not alone. In fact, in a story published by the *Wall Street Journal* titled "The

Morningstar Mirage,"[vii] research highlighted just how common and problematic this practice can be.

In their story, the authors point directly to Morningstar's popular 5-star rating system and the funds that attain the coveted status of being named a 5-star fund. It then follows how those same funds perform in periods subsequent to earning the rating—and the results aren't positive. Dating back to 2003, only 12% of funds earning the 5-star rating performed well enough over their next 5 years to earn the rating again. Worse yet, 10% actually performed so poorly that they were downgraded to a 1-star rating in the period immediately following. While Morningstar contends that their star rating was never intended to predict future performance—rather just to show backward-looking results—the takeaway is clear. An investment's past performance is completely independent of how it may perform going forward. In fact, based on the research, an investor could actually improve the odds of picking an outperformer by eliminating 5-star funds from the universe of consideration entirely!

Don't misrepresent past performance:
Proper asset allocation, rebalancing, and discipline are key. With proper planning and the identification of a target allocation (i.e., the mix of stocks and bonds in your portfolio), you can use a disciplined process of rebalancing to ensure your portfolio

remains in alignment with its original objective. This process also helps guard against the risk of chasing fad investments or recent top performers.

Assume you identify that a target mix of 70% stock/30% bonds is appropriate for your age and financial situation. In the following year, the stock market performs extremely well. Upon checking your portfolio at year end, you find it has drifted to resemble more of an 80% stock/20% bond mix due to the growth of the stock investments relative to bonds. Rather than leave the allocation as status quo (which would increase its risk), you could sell out of stocks and buy bonds so that your portfolio returns to its initial target mix. Conversely, in periods of stock market volatility, rather than simply riding it out, you would be buying stocks and selling bonds, as a means to bring your portfolio back into alignment.

The process of executing this strategy over time accomplishes two primary goals:

1. By keeping the portfolio allocation in alignment, the risk of the portfolio remains consistent with your needs and objectives.
2. The process of rebalancing in this manner can provide the framework for trading decisions that force a disciplined buy-low/sell-high approach. In other words, as a result of selling outperformers because they

have grown too large in the portfolio, you're making a decision based on the numbers, not emotion. You then would also be purchasing recent underperformers that otherwise may not be in favor but stand to do well in the near future.

Even for strong minds, investing and the game of golf can provide enough challenges to keep you on your toes. Don't become your own worst enemy by letting emotion and behavioral biases interfere with what logic and reason tell you to do.

Hole #3: Pick Clubs that Fit — Know the Investments You're Working With

"Hit the shot you know you can hit, not the one you think you should." —Dr. Bob Rotella, sports psychologist

Some of my earliest golf memories date back to when I was just 5 years old. Because my dad is a lefty, I wasn't able to use any of his hand-me-downs, so I usually ended up swinging the clubs that my older cousins had outgrown. Often just a little too big for me at the outset, I grew into them eventually—but they always took some adjusting to. That is, until the summer I turned 8 years old.

The summer I turned 8, my parents decided it was time to let me have a set of golf clubs that were my very own—a set just for me—and we headed to Charlie's house for me to get measured and fit. Charlie is legendary in my hometown. He was the person who everyone turned to when needing a club adjustment or new, custom-made equipment. He was also known to walk our home course with no golf bag, carrying only a 5-iron and a putter, capable still of beating most low-handicappers carrying a full set of clubs. I remember standing in the hallway of his home, back against a door frame in his living room, as he placed a pencil mark measuring my height and adding *my* initials among the countless

31

others that had stood in that very same spot. Measurements in hand, we reviewed the available options from his club catalog and selected a model that he would get to work on.

The anticipation over the following weeks, as I counted down the days until my clubs were ready, could most closely be approximated by the feeling of a 5-year-old on Christmas Eve. When the clubs finally arrived, the pride I felt as I hit practice shot after practice shot at the mulch beds surrounding the trees in my backyard was immeasurable. I had a set of clubs that were built just for me. A perfect fit!

In golf, consistency is the name of the game. Being able to repeat swings with consistent outcomes is the difference between good golfers and great ones; and a major factor impacting a golfer's ability to perform consistently is knowing the clubs in his or her bag. Understanding the advantages and disadvantages of each particular club allows the golfer to select the tool that is best capable of helping them achieve the distance, ball flight, and accuracy required to produce consistent shots that improve scoring ability.

In much the same way we think about the different clubs in our bag and which shot types each particular club is best designed to hit, different types of investments carry their own unique strengths and weaknesses. Their effectiveness is dependent upon the specific goals and objectives of your portfolio.

Risk and return are tied closely together. As we assume more risk, we expect to be compensated by way of earning a higher rate of return. The most common way of measuring risk in a portfolio is by evaluating its standard deviation. Of course, I wouldn't throw out a term you probably haven't heard since your high school statistics class without a golf analogy for explaining it, so think of standard deviation as the "spray probability" of your golf shots. Sure, you tend to hit the driver longer than your 7-iron, but it also tends to miss the fairway much more regularly. In contrast, while your ball doesn't travel as far when hit with your seven-iron, it much more frequently goes straighter and lands closer to its target.

This is similar to the risk/return relationship noted above. Let's assume you're standing on the tee box of the 18th hole: a 300-yard par 4, with trees up the left side and water all along the right. You're playing in a tournament and coming into the hole, you have a 1-shot lead. Would you hit driver and try to go for the green? Maybe. But, the higher probability shot would be to hit a shorter club to take the trouble out of play. Would your decision be different if you were 2 shots down? Probably. Think about why this is. The driver provides you with an opportunity to reach the green and putt for eagle (high return), but also a higher probability of missing your target and hitting it into trouble (high risk). Conversely, with an iron in hand, there's very little chance of reaching the green off the tee and making eagle (low return), but also a good probability you'll be hitting your approach from the middle of the fairway (low risk). Think of standard deviation then as the likelihood of a shot straying from its target. High standard deviation implies a greater probability of missing its target, whereas low standard deviation implies landing pretty close to it each time.

With that understanding in mind, how can the concepts of risk and return be applied to better assemble the investments within your portfolio? By thinking of investment asset classes as the different types of golf clubs in your bag, you can build an understanding of which are most appropriate for you to include in your portfolio. In particular:

Stocks: The Long Hitters

What is a stock? Sure, you may be familiar with ticker symbols and the stock-picking game you played in high school. But think about the question for a moment: What is a stock? In reality, when you purchase a stock you are purchasing fractional ownership in an underlying company. Stock is initially issued as a way for company owners to raise capital and, hopefully, enable that company to expand and grow. In exchange for capital that is provided to the company, the company sells a portion of itself and a claim to its future earnings to the shareholder.

We tend to think of the stock market as the consummate what-have-you-done-for-me-lately game. In fact, it's not just what have you done for me lately, but rather what will you do for me next? As stock owners, we derive value from the earnings that a company will return to us and as a result, the key factor that drives a stock's price is its expected *future* earnings.

When comparing two stocks, the expectation of higher future earnings should command a higher stock price, all else being equal. And further, as expectations about those earnings change, so will the assessment of value. Expect the costs of fertilizer to skyrocket over the next 5 years? I imagine we'd have to reassess the amount we'd be willing to pay to purchase our local golf course. Expect the cost of graphite to drop over the next five years? Perhaps the outlook for golf club manufacturers may be improving. The point is, as a shareholder, you are entitled to a proportionate claim of the profits generated by the company you own; as a company's ability to generate profits changes, so will the price of its stock.

A second major variable that will impact a stock's price is perceived future risk. That's because, as the owner of a company, you're exchanging the certainty of what you have today for the *expectation* of greater value in the future and, as you well know, the future for any company is uncertain. To compensate for accepting this tradeoff, you require to earn a return on your investment—the higher the expected risk, the higher the return required.

Much like the driver in your golf bag, stocks can be risky. You may launch a drive 300 yards down the middle or you may slice it 225 yards into the weeds. In the world of stocks, you may be investing in a company that will be the first to successfully unveil a golf ball that can be tracked with a GPS chip, but it may also spend its way into oblivion prior to being able to bring the concept to fruition.

For the risk that is being assumed by investing in the stock of a company, there is an expectation of a higher return than is associated with other types of investments such as cash or bonds. That said, stocks play a very important role in your portfolio. Just as it may be nearly impossible to reach a par-5 in regulation if the only club in your bag is a pitching wedge, excluding stocks entirely because of their associated risk can prolong the time required to achieve your goals. However, when used prudently and with a good understanding of the expected risk/return associated, stocks can provide a tremendous boost to your financial plan.

Putter: The Stroke Saver When Things Go Awry
If stocks are the long hitters of your portfolio, then bonds should most definitely be considered your putter. In most rounds of golf (especially those I play), shots will go awry from time to time. Maybe it's an errant tee shot that leaves you playing from the tall grass. Or an off-line approach shot that leaves a 50-foot putt for par. No matter how bad things go, your putter can always save serious strokes over the course of a round.

A similar phenomenon happens when investing. No matter how carefully you plan, market pullbacks are inevitable and when they happen, the value of your investment portfolio will fall. And while it is still reasonable to expect stocks to provide a superior long-term return, how you capitalize on pullbacks can be the difference between getting to the clubhouse under par and limping in as the high-handicapper of your group.

Take 2008 for example. The mere mention of the year is enough to send shivers down the spines of those who were approaching retirement, forced to watch as the value of stock markets plummeted in a manner not experienced since the Great Depression. But maybe it didn't need to be that scary. What if, instead of looking at the period as the greatest crash since the 1920s, you were able to view it as the greatest opportunity of your lifetime?

How so? Only if bonds were a part of your portfolio would you have had the flexibility to execute.

From January 1, 2008 to December 31, 2008, nearly all asset classes and sectors experienced significant losses. The S&P 500 was down 37%, international developed markets[viii] were off 43%, real estate[ix] was down 38%, and emerging markets[x] were down by more than 50%. Even so, there was an asset class that actually increased in value over that same period, to the tune of 5%. Bonds[xi]. While the rest of the market crashed, bonds actually increased in value.

When a company issues a bond, it is issuing a promise to repay a certain amount of money within a certain period of time and then securing that promise (in most cases) with a claim to specific assets. A company issuing a bond is, in many ways, similar to that of an individual purchasing an asset financed by debt. Take purchasing a home, for example. You want to buy a certain home, but don't currently have enough cash in your checking account to purchase it outright. Therefore, you approach a bank and the bank lends you the money to purchase the home in exchange for your promise to repay it.

By comparison, when a company issues a bond, it's generally because said company wants to acquire an asset but doesn't have readily available cash to do so. Therefore, in exchange for a promise to repay a certain amount, it sells bonds to investors who, in turn, loan money to the company. The primary difference between being a bond owner vs. a stockowner—and why the risk is lower for bond owners—is that the former are higher on the ladder in regard to when they receive payment. The interest (and often principal) that is owed to a bondholder is required to be paid before any income (or dividends) could be paid to owners of the company's stock. Because of the lower risk, bond owners are compensated with lower rates of return for their investments.

While bonds can indeed outperform stocks in certain periods, such as the 2008 example noted above, they can also be plagued by challenges similar to those of holding too much cash in a portfolio; excess safety may sacrifice needed return. Accordingly, it is important to determine an appropriate mix of bonds to hold within a portfolio that will help provide stability and purchasing power in the midst of market downturns, without unnecessarily prolonging the amount of time required to achieve your goals. (On Hole #4, we'll focus on the getting this mix just right.)

Hybrids: Custom Shots for Specific Situations
Not quite a long iron, not really a fairway wood, hybrids are clubs that take many different forms. Hybrids may be quite practical for some golfers, but

many find them to serve a very limited role and merely an added cost in the bag.

Like hybrids for golfers, there are a number of additional asset classes available to investors. But, also like a hybrid, you should fully understand how they are structured and if they may be of benefit to your situation before including them in your portfolio.

1. Real estate: By and large, real estate can often be an excellent addition to a portfolio, as it tends to exhibit an independent relationship from stocks and bonds. The result is, when used correctly and combined with stocks and bonds in a portfolio, real estate can increase the level of diversification. Real estate also tends to be a relatively high, stable income generator given the structure of most investment real estate (for example, rental properties). Even so, real estate is certainly not without its unique set of risks.

When investing in real estate, it's extremely important to consider the diversity of the investment (location, types of property owned, number of properties owned, etc.) to ensure you're not overly concentrated in any particular property. Additionally, be aware of the amount of leverage or debt that is being used to finance the purchase. While leverage can certainly enhance the return of an investment on the upside, it magnifies losses should an investment go south.

A subset of real estate investments, known as real estate investment trusts (a.k.a., REITs), are structured in a manner similar to mutual funds and can act to spread investor cash flow across multiple properties, geographic regions, and property types. On the surface, the diversification benefit of REITs is a positive; if electing to use these investments, however, you need to be very aware of their sales structure. Far too often, REITs are peddled by brokers being paid very high commissions to push a product with excessive fees and lengthy lockup periods, which potentially eliminates much of the benefit of owning the asset. To help protect against this, look for REITs that trade publicly on stock exchanges and come without any sales loads. Finally, ensure that you consider the tax implications of the high income that REITs generate. If possible, and permissible by the IRS for your specific investment, consider owning REITs in a tax-advantaged account such as an IRA or 401(k). By doing so, you can defer taxes on the income generated as opposed to paying the IRS each year.

2. Commodities: Just like hybrids in your golf bag, the term commodities can be taken to represent a multitude of different types of materials, from corn and soybeans to natural gas and oil, to precious metals like gold and silver. Although each may provide a hedging benefit in certain types of markets, it's extremely important to note that commodities, unlike the companies that procure them, do not generate an income stream themselves: the only means for a commodity to increase in value is by way of changes in supply and demand (including speculation). Therefore, before deciding to own commodities in your portfolio, I would encourage you to ask yourself why you are choosing to do so and if there may be a more efficient means to that end. While commodities may provide a hedge in severe down markets, in the majority of instances, commodities (gold in particular) can act to increase taxes, reduce income, and create drag on your portfolio's returns.

3. Cash: Ever had one of those rounds where simply nothing seemed to go your way? Tee shots go out of bounds, there's more sand in your golf shoes than your beach sandals, and even the shots that land in the fairway seem to have a side-hill lie. In the middle of a round like that, I've often wondered if I would have scored better using nothing other than my putter. Of course, this doesn't work in reality, much in the same way holding *excess* cash in your portfolio may prevent you from reaching your goals on time. There's simply *too much* safety involved.

While it is certainly a good idea to hold some cash out of the market as an emergency fund[xii], having too much cash in a portfolio is like hitting a putter from the tee box. Sure, you have a clear idea of where it's going to go, but it also won't go far.

Many investors elect to hold cash because they believe it carries very little risk. While cash may have very little *volatility*, in the context of losing purchasing power, cash may very well be the riskiest asset of all. Because the return of cash generally trails that of inflation, it essentially guarantees a loss of purchasing power, which is compounded over the long term. It's far better to take some risk to earn a higher rate of return and mentally prepare to capitalize when things don't go according to plan than to take no risk and guarantee an inefficient path to meeting your goals.

Equipped with an understanding of the different types of investments available, how can this information assist you in determining how much of each to hold in your portfolio? On the next hole, we'll focus on doing just that!

Hole #4: Asset Allocation — What's in the Bag?

"If I had to choose between my wife and my putter, well, I'd miss her"—Gary Player

What if I told you there was a single factor—just one—that was responsible for determining more than 90% of your portfolio's return[xiii]? Think that factor would be picking the right stocks? Nope. Being able to time the market? Not even close. What about having access to sophisticated investment strategies and getting in on hot IPOs? Not that either.

When it comes to driving a portfolio's return, evidence suggests that asset allocation—the mix of asset classes included within your portfolio—is the single largest factor in determining long-term results. In fact, as alluded to above, asset allocation has been shown to determine upwards of 90% of a portfolio's total return! Further, research also suggests that by emphasizing other factors—trying to time the market, pick the next high-flying stock, or chase top-performing funds/fund managers—investors may actually reduce the return their portfolio is able to generate over time[xiv]. Think about that for a moment. How much time does a typical investor spend trying to decide which companies to own? Or if now is a good time to invest cash vs. waiting for the next pullback? How many investment clubs dedicate their efforts to analyzing companies they believe are going to outperform in the coming year? In reality, the research tells us that these efforts not only waste time, but also negatively impact results. So instead let's focus on where we can drive the most value and maximize both our return on time *and* investment.

I realize Phil Mickelson isn't the only golfer on tour to change the types of clubs he carries from one tournament to the next, but he does seem to be the most creative. For example, at the 2017 Open Championship, Phil elected not to carry a driver at all. Instead, he decided that two 3-irons and four wedges were better options for the course. Contrast that with his bag at The Masters, where he didn't carry a 3-iron at all and instead included a 5-wood, utility club, and driver in his arsenal. Phil does for his golf game what investors should be doing for their portfolios: customizing. That is, he understands how his particular strengths and weaknesses may interact with the challenges and playing conditions of a given golf course. He then tailors his available club selection to ensure he puts himself in the best possible position to succeed.

When it comes to customizing an investment portfolio, there are a few critical areas that should be intimately understood to ensure the portfolio is best positioned to attack your financial goals at hand. These include:

Consideration #1: Emotional Risk Tolerance (i.e., ability to handle the market's swings): John Maynard Keynes once said that the market can stay irrational much longer than we can stay solvent. How true! The only certainty when it comes to investing is that future market movements are uncertain. The market rises and the market falls. Talking heads on TV and various media outlets will often attempt to explain "why," but the truth is, usually no one really knows—and certainly no one is able to predict its movements in advance. Consider the following chart (Chart 1 - S&P 500 Annual Performance, 1980-2017):

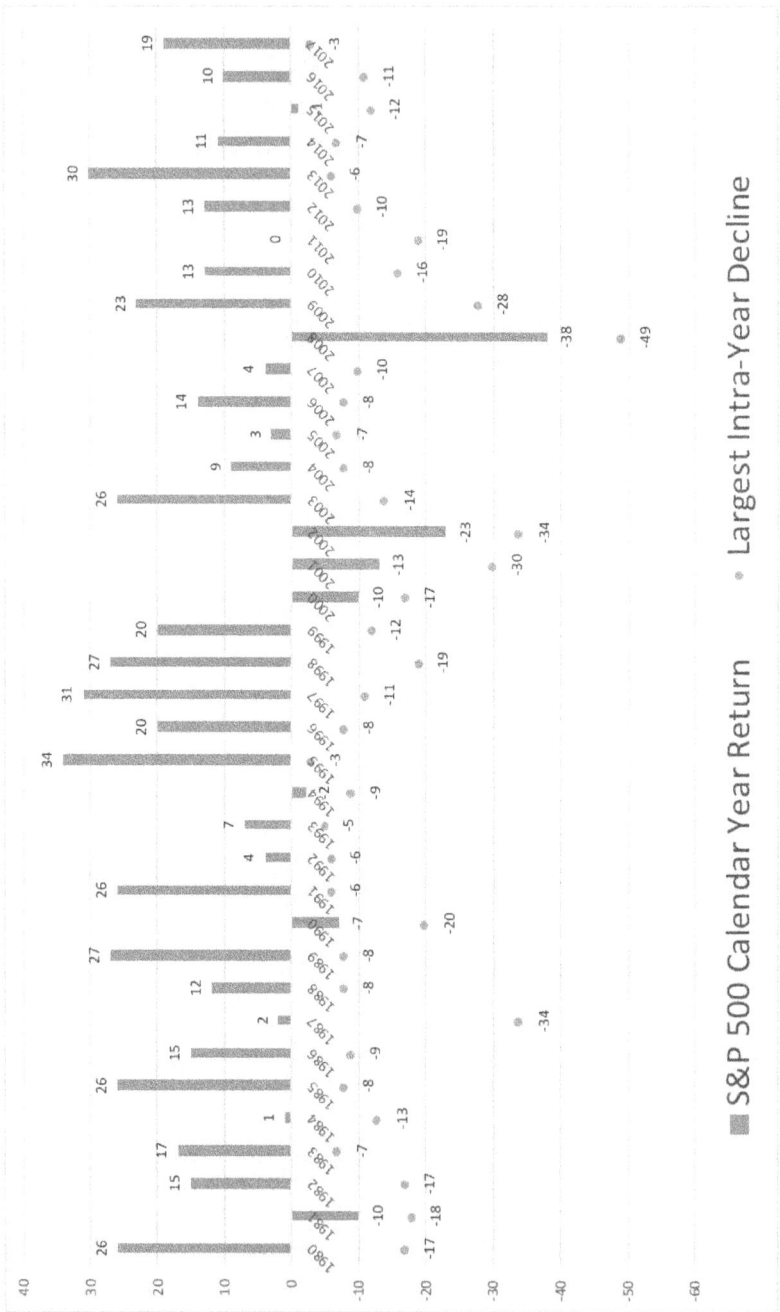

S&P 500 Calendar Year Return   • Largest Intra-Year Decline

Chart 1 references two contrasting data points related to the performance of the S&P 500 going back to 1980. The bars on the chart detail the annual performance of the S&P 500 for the respective calendar year: In other words, if you bought the index on January 1 and did nothing, on December 31 you would have earned the return detailed. The dots in the chart, by contrast, highlight the maximum pullback within a given year. For example, at some point in the year 2010, the S&P 500 experienced a decline of 16%. However, investors who were able to drown out the noise, remaining invested from January 1–December 31, would still have earned a return for the year of 13%.

As the chart shows, volatility is a very natural part of the stock market—but that doesn't necessarily mean that every person is 100% comfortable with it. Dating back to 1980, the S&P 500 has generated a positive annual return more than 76% of the time. However, even the positive years experienced an average intra-year decline of 13.3%. While the positive returns throughout the years proved very beneficial for the investors that were able to stay committed, it could prove catastrophic for those who lost faith in the midst of a decline.

Knowing that market volatility is natural and recurring can be a powerful tool in helping investors plan to stay committed year in and year out. But, as Mike Tyson once said, "Everyone has a plan till they get punched in the mouth." Be honest with yourself in assessing your level of comfort with market volatility. How did you react in the 2008–2009 market declines? What about 2016 when the S&P 500 began with its worst-ever start to a year? While our behaviors can change over time, often our best indicator of future action is how we've reacted in the recent past. If you're electing to get more aggressive with your investment portfolio, ensure you're making a commitment for the long term. Otherwise, you risk falling into the recurring cycle of buying in periods of market exuberance and high prices, only to turn around and sell out when the market turns negative – and buy high, sell low, repeat until it's gone was never a strategy that worked out well for anyone!

Consideration #2: Time Horizon (i.e., the amount of time until access to investments is required):

Over short periods of time in particular, markets can be extremely unpredictable. We do not know when the next market correction may happen, but we do know that it *will* happen. How you react in the midst of such pullbacks will go a long way towards making or breaking your financial plan.

As described above, investors who are uncomfortable with temporary declines in their portfolios may consider holding a reduced level of riskier assets. The same principle applies to investors with very limited time horizons (i.e., a short period of time until cash is needed), for the exact same reason: avoiding a forced sale in the face of market weakness.

a. As a first step, investors should plan on building an emergency cash account to prevent from having to dip into debt to cover expenses due to job loss, or urgent home or car repairs. A good target for married couples who are both working would be 3 to 6 months' worth of living expenses. For singles, or single-income households, a good target is 6 to 9 months, given the larger shock a job loss would cause.

b. Additionally, if there are known needs of cash in the short term (say within 18 to 24 months at a minimum), it would be best to keep this money parked in a checking or savings account. Reason being, even if you are the most risk-on investor and use every pullback as an opportunity to pile into stocks every time they go on sale, market research suggests that a market correction (i.e., pullback of at least 10%) happens, on average, every other year. By keeping short term needs in cash accounts, investors can avoid having to decide between selling investments in the midst of a temporary decline or forgoing a dream golf trip due to funds that evaporated in the market.

Consideration #3: Return Requirements (i.e., the return needed to meet your goals): Ever heard someone described as having "champagne tastes and a beer budget"? It's a phrase intended to point out the obvious mismatch between the new golf clubs we'd like to purchase and the funds available to spend on said purchase. The same can often apply to financial plans in the context of goals we hope to achieve, the level of assets required to achieve them, and the investment risk willing to be accepted to get there.

As mentioned earlier, the relationship of risk and return is tightly intertwined. We can expect stocks to produce higher long-term returns relative to bonds (and certainly cash), but we also must be willing to accept a bumpier ride along the way. Accordingly, when evaluating financial goals and the assets that are required to reach them, it is critical to ensure that the return you expect is reasonably consistent with the asset mix of your portfolio. As a point of reference, consider the following chart[xv]:

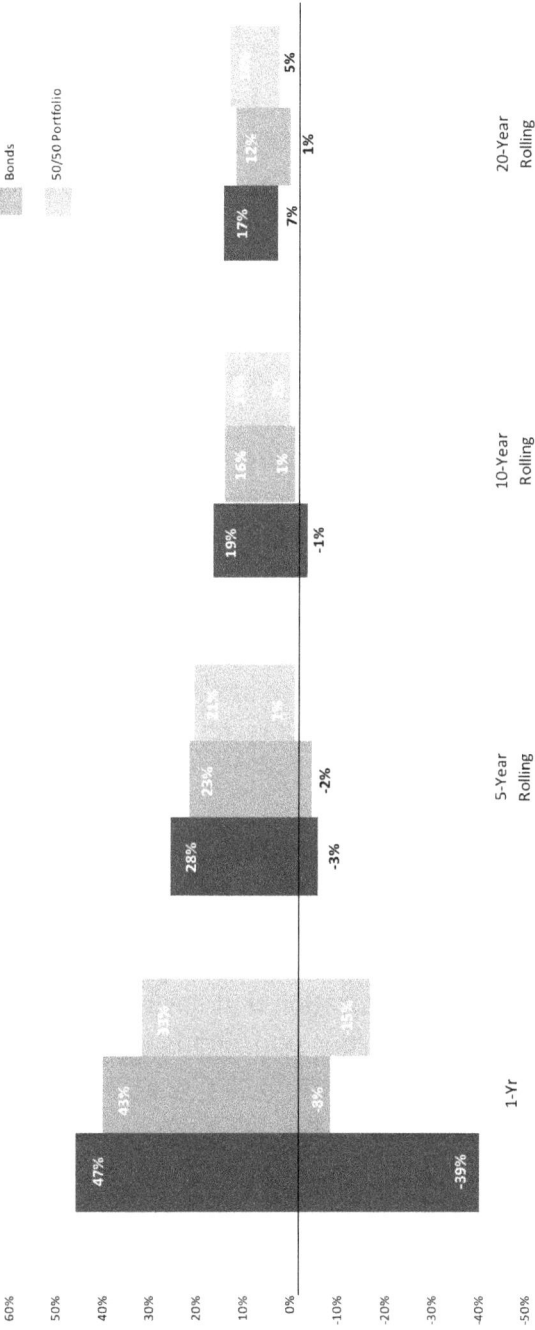

Range of stock, bond, and blended total returns
Annual total returns, 1950 - 2017

Legend: Stocks · Bonds · 50/50 Portfolio

Axis: 60%, 50%, 40%, 30%, 20%, 10%, 0%, -10%, -20%, -30%, -40%, -50%

1-Yr: Stocks 47% / -39%; Bonds 43% / -8%; 50/50 Portfolio 33% / -15%

5-Year Rolling: Stocks 28% / -3%; Bonds 23% / -2%; 50/50 Portfolio 21% / 1%

10-Year Rolling: Stocks 19% / -1%; Bonds 16% / 1%

20-Year Rolling: Stocks 17% / 7%; Bonds 12% / 1%; 50/50 Portfolio 5%

In summary, this chart details the maximum and minimum returns of a 100% stock allocation, a 100% bond allocation, and a blended 50% stock/50% bond allocation over rolling 1-, 5-, 10-, and 20-year periods dating back to 1950. It's obvious that in short periods of time stocks can be extremely volatile. The best 1-year return for stocks is 47%, but their worst single year saw a decline of -39%. Bonds, by contrast, are much less likely to suffer significant declines from year to year -- ranging from positive 43% in their best single year to down 8% in their worst. Over an extended time-horizon, however, stocks have fared significantly better, providing much higher returns as compensation for the volatility that was assumed. In fact, dating all the way back to 1950, there has never been a 20-year period over which stocks returned any less than 7%[xvi]!

While certainly not a perfect indicator—remember, "past performance doesn't reflect future results"— the above chart can be a useful guide in assessing whether the return expectations for your portfolio align with the allocation that has been settled into. For example, if your portfolio is invested 100% in bonds, it's likely unreasonable to expect an average long-term return of 10% per year.

Putting it all together: Constructing an investment MAP

Understanding the importance of asset allocation is a powerful first step in portfolio construction, but how does it all fit together when there are real dollars to be invested? To provide some context for putting together your own portfolio, I've created an approach that you can use to begin building a portfolio that will align with your goals: a MAP for your investment plan.

The MAP approach to portfolio construction breaks down different types of investments (based upon their risk/return characteristics) into three distinct buckets. It then aligns the percentage of assets held in each bucket with the timeline of specific financial goals. For example, a young investor with 10+ years until needing access to their investments may hold a very high percentage of assets in the Multiply bucket and a very limited amount in the Assure bucket. By contrast, an investor who is planning to retire this year may hold a relatively small amount of assets in the Multiply bucket, but a large percentage in the Assure and Paycheck buckets to provide for current, near-term income needs.

Bucket 1: <u>**MULTIPLY**</u>—The Multiply bucket focuses on the portfolio's growth prospects and would generally be invested in stocks with higher growth potential. This bucket will tend to be the most volatile portion of the portfolio, but is key to growing the portfolio's principal over time. The amount of money that should be held in this bucket should be proportionate to the amount of time until access to the principal is required. (Longer time until cash is needed would correspond with greater dollar amounts housed in this bucket and vice versa.) Typically, funds in the Multiply bucket would be thought of as having at least 5+ years until being needed for use.

Bucket 2: **ASSURE**—The Assure bucket is dedicated to principal preservation and would generally be invested in lower risk assets, like bonds. As discussed previously, while bonds have historically underperformed stocks over the long term, their returns have been more stable as well. For this reason, the Assure bucket would be looked to as a way to rebalance the portfolio—i.e., buy stocks while they are on sale in the midst of a market downturn—or to provide capital to fund spending goals in the midst of market declines. To gauge the level of assets that should be held within the Assure bucket, look first to the level of spending required to be funded by the portfolio.

During the Great Recession, the S&P 500 fell from a high reached in October 2007 to a low in March 2009. However, perhaps even more problematic, was the fact that the S&P 500 did not again reach its pre-recession high until March of 2013 (nearly 5½ years later). Without leaving enough of a spending cushion in the Assure bucket, investors may have been forced to sell out of positions to continue funding their spending goals, in spite of their desire to do so.

Accordingly, as a means to protect against the risk of a forced sale of stocks, target a balance held within the Assure bucket of between 4 and 6 years' worth of living expenses. Investors who have greater flexibility with their spending (e.g., low/no mortgage, debt, or recurring obligations), can target the lower end of this range while investors with higher fixed expenses may want to target closer to the full 6 years.

Bucket 3: **PAYCHECK**—The Paycheck bucket focuses on the recurring income that a portfolio generates, independent of the price movements of the individual stocks or mutual funds in it. Think of a portfolio's income like the salary a job pays and price appreciation as a year-end bonus. That is, even if the price of a security is unchanged over the course of a year, if it has paid dividends, we've realized a positive benefit. In retirement, this income has the obvious benefit of covering spending goals on a relatively consistent basis. Prior to retirement, this income also can provide discretionary cash flow that can be used to invest across other parts of the portfolio (i.e., a rebalancing opportunity without having to sell any investments).

Income can and should be a key piece of the portfolio that can be customized to help efficiently meet goals—but should not necessarily be the *only* focus when it comes to selecting investments for inclusion. This is primarily because:

1. A focus exclusively on income ignores many great investment opportunities that may not yet be paying a dividend. It also ignores the impact of price appreciation, potentially sacrificing long-term growth. Within the S&P 500, there are a number of great companies that haven't yet started paying a dividend but have generated substantial returns for investors (Amazon, Google, and Facebook being the most notable). In fact, an investor who owned the S&P 500 index in 2017 minus those three stocks would have missed out on nearly 15% of the total return[xvii]!

2. If not held within a tax-advantaged account, such as a 401(k), IRA, or Roth, the income generated by investments is taxable each year. Therefore, all else equal, capital appreciation can provide more tax efficient growth for an investor relative to investment income. This is because an investor is able to decide when to buy/sell their investments (and therefore pay taxes), whereas income generated by investments is taxed each year—regardless of whether

the income is needed and spent or saved and re-invested.

By building an investment MAP and developing a strategy for the level of assets to hold in the various buckets, you can help ensure that your portfolio is in alignment with your financial plan. In turn, the strategy will help you achieve the growth required to meet your goals while also guarding against sudden investment shocks that may otherwise derail you along your way.

Hole #5: Diversification — Don't Just Carry a 7-Iron

"There is a close logical connection between the concept of a safety margin and the principle of diversification."—Benjamin Graham

As I mentioned in the introduction to this book, one of my all-time favorite movies is *Tin Cup*. At the risk of a plot-spoiler for those who haven't seen it, there's a famous scene in which the main character Roy McAvoy takes golf clubs from his bag one by one and begins snapping each of them over his leg, as he rants about the errant shots each of them had hit at one time or another. He continues on his tirade until every club in his bag is destroyed other than his ever-faithful 7-iron. As the movie plays out, McAvoy continues his round, and ultimately proceeds to shoot even par using only the single club. Sitting on the clubhouse patio after finishing the round, he asks of his rival, David Sims, "You ever shoot par with a 7-iron?"

Sims smiles as he smugly replies, "Why, hell Roy, it never even occurred to me to try."

In his rebuttal, David Sims makes the point that McAvoy's feat is senseless. Why would a golfer ever voluntarily put himself at an obvious disadvantage by carrying only a single club, when the rules of the game permit carrying 14? The game of golf is plenty challenging when played with a full arsenal of clubs in the bag. It would seem foolish to voluntarily make it even more difficult.

Diversification, as it's commonly said, is the only free lunch in investing. With diversification, assets can be spread across a range of *uncorrelated* investments—in other words, those that tend to move independently of one another, providing an opportunity to increase a portfolio's expected return while simultaneously reducing its volatility (i.e., risk). Given the risk/return benefits, when diversification is properly understood and employed correctly, it can be an extremely powerful tool. But how can you make it work to your advantage?

Diversification is not merely the number of different stocks or even stock funds that are owned in a portfolio, but rather the relationship and interaction each investment in the portfolio has with another. Take, for example, what happened to many investors during the tech bubble. It's March 2000 and Mr. Tech, like many, has done very well investing in his company's stock. Sensing that he is taking on too much risk by having all of his eggs in a single basket, he decides to diversify his holdings. To do so, he sells all of his company's stock and purchases the stock of the top 100 companies (as measured by market capitalization[xviii]) on the NASDAQ Exchange. Spreading his proceeds across 100 different companies, he thinks, will provide ample diversification. Imagine his surprise when the value of his portfolio falls by more than 60% over the next two years, not returning the level of his initial investment until nearly 15 years later!

It is extremely common to equate the level of a portfolio's diversification directly with the *number* of positions that it holds. If that's all it takes, how could Mr. Tech's portfolio of 100 different stocks cause such a poor outcome? Answer: correlation.

Again, the value of diversification doesn't specifically depend only on the number of investments that are held within a portfolio, but rather how they each *interact* with one another: a relationship referred to as correlation. Assets that are linked by similar risk factors will tend to respond similarly to the forces that may be driving a certain market condition or cycle.

Think of it like the loft on your golf club. If you had 14 different drivers, each with a 9-degree loft, the outcome of your shots would likely be relatively the same—even if you hit some better than others. In addition, while the driver may position you well off the tee, your short game and play out of the bunker would suffer. True diversification is deciding not to carry a bag full of drivers (or, in Roy McAvoy's case, only a 7-iron) but rather to carry a variety of clubs, each of a different length, loft, and lie angle. Because each club provides a trade-off between distance, accuracy, and utility, having a number of different options available, better positions you to be prepared for any shot the course may throw your way. Likewise, instead of focusing on the *quantity* of different investments in your portfolio, consider how common risk factors in the market may impact each investment specifically. When structured correctly, high levels of diversification benefit can be achieved while owning a relatively limited number of investments within the portfolio.

As discussed on Hole #3, market forces tend to impact major asset classes differently, causing the asset classes to hold low correlations with one another, especially over longer periods of time. Given that low correlation serves as the foundation of an effective diversification strategy, you can use your understanding of asset classes to begin building an investment portfolio that is truly diversified—as opposed to one that simply holds many different securities. The end result of combining assets with low or negative correlations is an opportunity to reduce the volatility of your portfolio overall and ultimately improve its expected risk-adjusted return.

Because we've already discussed the characteristics of each particular asset class on Hole #3, we won't revisit each of them here. However, one often overlooked diversification strategy that exists within an asset class that is worth noting is the distinction between domestic and international securities.

While my Ryder Cup allegiances will forever be entrenched with the USA in the game of golf, when electing to invest, research suggests that mixing domestic and international assets may produce superior, risk-adjusted results. Of the many benefits touted, some of the most notable statistics include:

1. Only 42% of global company value is within the United States—58% of investment opportunities are abroad[xix].
2. Based on research conducted by Fidelity, while U.S. stocks have had higher returns than overseas equities in aggregate for the past several years, prior to 2017, the best-performing stock market for each of the past 30 years had been located outside the United States.
3. Although many companies within the U.S. have a large international presence (e.g., Proctor and Gamble, Ford, Oracle, among countless others), these companies still tend to perform much more in line with the US stock market than those abroad—and therefore typically will not provide ample international diversification.
4. Fidelity also found that, in the post-World War II era, a portfolio composed of both US and international stocks carried a standard deviation that was nearly 10% lower than one invested entirely in the US.

There is power in diversification and, when used correctly, it can help improve your portfolio's risk/return dynamic. Rather than emphasize the number of investments in your portfolio, shift your focus to the mix and interaction those investments have within it. Doing so will put you well on the way to tackling any shot you might encounter on the course to financial independence!

Hole #6: Drive for Show, Putt for Dough — Active vs. Passive Investments

"Drive for Show, Putt for Dough"—Famous Golf Adage

To earn a score of par, golf rules allow for 2 putts upon reaching a green in regulation. But have you ever actually tracked the number of putts you hit over the course of a round? For the typical weekend player, it's probably fair to assume that 36 putts would be on the low end. So, for most of us, if a playing partner offered up every one of our putts inside 20 feet as a gimmie, there's no doubt our scores would improve.

In his book, *Every Shot Counts*, Dr. Mark Broadie charts numerous statistics and scoring probabilities frequently encountered in a round of golf. The concept of "strokes gained" (off the tee, on the green, etc.) that you hear TV golf analysts talk about was largely a product of Dr. Broadie's research. One particularly interesting finding was that only 15% of putts struck from a distance of 20 feet are actually made. Meaning, if we left ourselves a 20-footer 18 times in an 18-hole round, we would expect to sink less than 3 of them—and 15 or more would be two-putts or worse. (So, if you find a playing partner willing to concede your 20-foot putts, keep 'em in your weekly foursome!)

Transitioning to the world of investing, what if an investment was statistically shown to underperform its benchmark more than 85% of the time? In golf terms, you'd have better odds of making a 20-foot putt than this investment does of outperforming its benchmark. Not too favorable, right? In a study conducted by Research Affiliates' founder and chairman, Robert Arnott, the performance of 203 actively managed mutual funds with at least $100 million under management was tracked for a period of 15 years[xx] and his study's results showed just that.

In fact, the results of Arnott's study found that a remarkable 96% of the funds tracked failed to beat the market—*96%*!

With such staggering odds stacked against investors in these types of funds, it seems logical that they should be avoided at all costs. But what is an actively managed fund, and why do they notoriously perform so poorly? More importantly, what alternatives are available that may offer more favorable odds to investors?

Actively managed mutual funds are investments run by fund managers who have been tasked with a goal of beating the market. That is, the managers believe they have identified a particular strategy—stock picking, market timing, algorithmic trading, etc.— that is supposedly able to provide them an advantage that will translate into their fund outperforming the market overall.

In contrast, rather than attempting to outperform the market, passively managed investments merely try to match the return of an underlying index by proportionately owning the same securities of those in the index itself. Common examples of a passive fund would be those that track the S&P 500 for US stocks, the Barclays Aggregate Bond Index in the fixed income space, or the MSCI EAFE for international stocks.

On the surface, one would assume that professional stock pickers running exotic and sophisticated strategies would be capable of generating higher returns than their passively managed counterparts who purchase and hold the securities of a publicly available index. But as Arnott's study and other continued evidence suggests, the odds of this actually happening are far less than the odds of you sinking a 20-footer. Here's why:

1. **Fees matter a lot, but are often overlooked.** Consider the following example. Two investors each purchase an investment that is identical in every way except the fees. Investment 1 charges a management fee of 1%, whereas investment 2 charges a management fee of 2%. At the onset, $100,000 is invested in each fund and the

fund generates a return of 10% each year, prior to investment fees. Twenty-five years later, the two investors review their account statements and are shocked: Even though they had owned the same investments, the difference in fees (compounded over time) generated a difference in portfolio value of $177,000. Translated into spending terms, it could be the difference in retiring now vs. having to wait an extra 2 or 3 years!

Due to their so-called sophisticated strategies and higher overhead costs, actively managed funds typically carry an expense ratio that is much higher than their passively managed counterparts. As an example, let's use the ticker VOO. VOO is a fund from the Vanguard family that is designed to replicate the S&P 500. From its research page on Morningstar, we can see that the expense ratio of the fund is 0.05%, or $0.50 for every $1,000 invested in the fund. (The expense ratio is expressed in annual terms, so this is a recurring fee each year.) By comparison, the average mutual fund fee in the industry is 1.33%[xxi] —more than 26 times the expense ratio of VOO. And that is just the average! In golf terms, this difference is equivalent to the choice between purchasing a dozen Pro V1 golf balls for $48 or buying a round of golf for you *and a friend* at Pebble Beach for $1,200. Due to their higher cost structure, active funds are handicapped from the beginning.

2. **Markets are extremely efficient.** In *Flash Boys*, Michael Lewis tells the story of high-frequency trading and the extreme lengths and millions upon millions of dollars that are spent by trading firms to gain a *millisecond* advantage over others. For reference, it takes approximately 100 milliseconds to blink your eye. If we equate efficiency with the ability for markets to quickly and accurately incorporate all known information into a stock's price, then it may be an understatement to suggest that markets are anything but when one millisecond makes a difference.

   But why is that important? Because, if a stock's price already reflects all publicly available information (for better or worse) into its current trading price, then, absent being in possession of material non-public information[xxii], there is very little opportunity for that stock to produce surprise value or excess return. It's the reason that great companies don't always make great stocks, as measured by their return relative to others, and vice versa.

Market prices are set by aggregating the collective opinions of its participants. All participants have an opinion as to what a stock's true value is, and the market simply translates those collective opinions into a price that buyers and sellers agree to. The seller is dumping a stock at what they believe is an overvalued price, which the buyer thinks is a bargain pickup.

To help demonstrate, let's say you were to play a round of golf against Dustin Johnson and the world was permitted to gamble on the outcome. Unless you're a pro golfer who happens to be reading this, there would be very few people willing to bet that you would win this match. In terms of the stock market, Dustin represents a superior company. To facilitate action in the market, gamblers begin handicapping the match by offering up shots to incentivize bets to be placed on you, changing the price of the stock. At first, it may require you getting an extra 7 shots per side to get others to bet on your victory, maybe more, maybe less. At some point, the odds start to level, and Dustin's talent edge begins to fade away. Now imagine that you and Dustin were frequent playing partners, and the margin of victory for each of your matches had been charted and was publicly available to anyone wanting to get in on the action. The introduction of all of this information is incorporated into the margin of strokes offered and is so statistically precise that the odds of one golfer winning vs. the other is little other than pure chance.

This is essentially the same process through which the stock market operates. Instead of strokes, the market uses pricing. The market combines the expectations and information known by all investors, analysts, stock pickers, etc., and collectively aggregates it all into a price. To gain an edge that would enable an investor to pick stocks that would outperform those expectations, he or she would need to have legal knowledge that was not yet reflected by the market *and* be able to quickly act upon that knowledge. In reality, given the millions of participants in the market and the ability of computers to process information in less than 1/100th the amount of time it takes to blink an eye, the odds of investors successfully and *consistently* being able to do so essentially becomes a coin flip -- or worse.

A logical follow-up question is: "If even professional stock pickers can't pick outperformers, what's the sense in investing at all?" ***The answer is important: Simply because we may not be able to consistently beat the market, doesn't mean that the market*** *itself can't provide a great return.* After all, the S&P 500 has generated an average return of 11.2% per year dating all the way back to 1950. I'll take that, and I bet you would too. Fortunately, as mentioned earlier in this chapter, there is a subset of investments tasked with the goal of tracking those market returns. And they're quickly growing in popularity.

Due to their simplified structure, passive investments offer some major advantages to investors. Most notably they include a reduced cost structure, typically a fraction of the cost of their actively traded counterparts. And because these funds own the same stocks that are held within an index, there is limited risk that one will miss out on owning its top performers. Two additional key advantages passive funds maintain relative to their actively traded counterparts include:

1. **Reduced cash drag:** In an investment fund, cash drag is like hitting a tee shot into the wind. Cash weighs on a fund's performance as a result of the very low return it is capable of generating. Because active managers are typically focused on trying to pick the next hot stock or time the next market pullback, they often keep excess cash waiting on the sidelines. Over time, this weighs on the performance of the fund. By contrast, a passive investment is merely looking to own

the same securities that exist in the index itself. Therefore, a passive investment is able to remain much more fully invested over time, as changes to an index are customarily few and far between, (and also widely publicized). This acts to ensure more of your investment is working for you, as opposed to sitting on the sidelines waiting to get into the game.

2. **Taxes.** Fund companies do not directly pay taxes on the gains realized from their underlying holdings. They rely on fund owners to do that by kicking out tax distributions to be included in year-end tax returns. Moreover, these gains are distributed to fund owners as of a particular date of record, which may not necessarily be the same person that owned the fund when the gains were actually realized. Like a game of alternate shot, when you could be forced to play your partner's tee shot out of the tall grass, this means that you could potentially inherit the tax liability of someone else's gains, regardless of whether you've actually experienced any appreciation in the price of your investment.

As their name implies, active managers tend to be more aggressive about trading securities within their fund. This increases the probability that taxes on gains may be at short-term rates (i.e., ordinary income) as opposed to the lower, long-term capital gains rates. Passive investments, by contrast, tend to have much less turnover from buying and selling, which results in improved tax efficiency for their investors.

In summary, relative to their actively traded counterparts, passive funds are typically associated with reduced costs, improved tax efficiency, and better returns. When these investments are coupled with certain trading strategies and a mind prepared to weather a bad hole, the odds of improving the overall outcome and efficiency of your round will improve significantly.

Hole #7: Learn to Play from the Hazard

"Of all the hazards, fear is the worst."—Sam Snead

Flash back for a moment to the 2017 Open Championship. Tied for the lead heading to the 13th tee, Jordan Spieth blocked his tee shot *way* right. Fortunate to even find his ball at all, Spieth was forced to take an unplayable lie, find a location to drop, and somehow not blow up his entire tournament effort on this single hole. Though it took nearly 30 minutes for Spieth to play his next shot, he was able to somehow scramble and escape with only a bogey on the scorecard. He went on from there to ultimately win the entire tournament.

If you play the game long enough, you come to realize that bad breaks are simply a part of it. Even in the midst of a great round, there will be shots that don't bounce your way, putts that lip out, or swing kinks that send an errant shot into a hazard. It's inevitable and, as the example above demonstrates, even the best players in the world are not immune. But what separates professionals from amateurs is an understanding that success is less about what has just happened and all about how you respond.

I'm sure the feeling in Jordan Spieth's stomach as he watched his tee shot on the 13th sail further and further away from the fairway wasn't all that different from the one you experience logging in to view your investment account in the midst of a market downturn. Nothing but big red numbers— down lower from yesterday and even further from the day before that. It's a sickening feeling to experience, but the professionals know, what's done is done. Whether a bad tee shot or a bad run in the market, there's nothing that can change the position we're now in. However, an unplayable lie today can be turned into a personal victory tomorrow. If you understand how to take advantage and can keep your focus on the bigger goal, a temporary disadvantage can become a great opportunity.

For anyone who is considering getting invested in the stock market, there is a concept that must be accepted and understood in order to have any level of success at all: *Volatility is a natural part of the market.* On the PGA Tour, even the best of the best will hit bad shots in every round they play. Yet, in most of those rounds, they still find a way to score under par for the day. It is in much the same way that the market will experience pullbacks within a given year but, more often than not, provide positive returns for the year overall. (Revisit Chart #1 on Hole #4.)

But let's take it one step further. Assume for a minute that, due to rotten luck, you chose the worst time in the past 20 years to invest a $100,000 lump sum of cash. That's right, you put $100,000 to work in October of 2007. Then, miraculously, you were able to avoid all news and social media for the next 10 years. Blissfully ignorant of the recession and market collapse that had transpired, after the 10-year period, you would have logged in to review your account and observe that your balance had grown to nearly $170,000[xxiii] . Wait, what?! That's right, you picked the absolute worst time to invest a lump sum of cash and upon checking your balance 10 years later, simply saw that it had grown by nearly 5.5% *each year*. That's the power of simply drowning out the noise.

Understanding that volatility is a natural part of the market and using that understanding to enable yourself to stay committed is a great start—buy and hold will typically fare much better than buy high, sell low. But down markets also create opportunities, and those opportunities can allow you to do better than merely riding it out. Instead you can capitalize on the market's weakness to improve your long-term situation. Consider the following examples that can help do just that.

Taking advantage when the market lands in a bunker: Market corrections, as they are commonly referred to, imply a drop in the market of 10% or more. Bear markets imply market drops of 20% or more. It's reasonable to want to avoid the pain associated with market corrections (and especially bear markets) but there can be a significant cost to doing so. As noted earlier, each year, on average, the market will experience a correction-level pullback of 13.8%. However, as also noted earlier, less than two out of five corrections will actually turn into a bear market.

See where I'm going with this? If we try and time the market to get out each time there's a 5% or 10% decline in the market, we may very well be jumping out just before the market recovers. In fact, if only two in five corrections actually turn into bear markets, the statistics would imply that we're actually better off using these opportunities to *add* to our positions—rather than jump out. The key here is to have a portfolio that is diversified well enough to provide sufficient capital (that has either maintained value or increased in value during the stock market sell off) that can be used to take advantage.

A great strategy to enable such execution is to have a pre-decided asset allocation that aligns with your long-term goals. (See Hole #4 for more detail on accomplishing this.) As the market sells off, driving stock prices down, those seeking safety drive up the value of bonds, and your portfolio mix starts to drift. The result is that bonds begin to increase as a percentage of your overall mix while the stock allocation declines. This can be used as an opportunity: not to speculate or try to pick the market's bottom, but rather to simply rebalance the portfolio, bringing it back into alignment with the original targets that were set. The simple math of following this strategy would cause the sale of bonds at high prices and the purchase of stocks on sale.

The end result? Once the market recovers, not only would your original positions recoup their value, but those that were acquired on the cheap would appreciate even more rapidly—allowing your positions to recover more quickly than the market itself. Think of rebalancing in both good times and bad as a disciplined way of forcing a sell-high/buy-low decision.

Taking free (tax) relief: As specified in the USGA's Rules of Golf, Rule 25-1.b permits a player whose ball has landed in an abnormal ground condition to take relief, without penalty from the condition. So, when our perfectly hit tee shot comes to a stop directly in the middle of the fairway, in yesterday's rain puddle, you're allowed to move the ball out of the puddle without having to add a penalty stroke: free relief.

The IRS has its own type of Rule 25-1.b, useful for investors in the midst of a market pullback. Schedule D of tax form 1040 reports the capital gains that investors have realized on the sale of their investments over the course of a year. This same schedule nets out capital losses from those gains as well: The amount of gain that is included on a tax return is reduced by any capital losses that may have also been realized. And, if there are only capital losses available to report, such losses can often be used to offset a portion of ordinary income. Excess losses can even be carried forward to use in future years. The moral of the story is that capital losses can be an extremely powerful tool since they provide a means of reducing your overall tax liability. But what does all of this have to do with taking advantage of a market pullback?

Tax-loss harvesting is a strategy whereby an investment is sold at a loss such that the loss can be captured (i.e., "harvested") to include on your tax return. Rather than holding the proceeds from the sale in cash and missing the subsequent market recovery, however, you would elect to purchase a *similar* security to replace the one that was sold. Because the IRS imposes restrictions (referred to as "wash-sale" rules) that prohibit the sale and purchase of an identical or "substantially" identical security within a period of 30 days, great care should be taken to ensure the securities being exchanged are different enough to meet the IRS's qualifications, yet similar enough to maintain the overall risk profile of the original portfolio.

Traditionally, tax loss harvesting will work best with a portfolio composed of index funds or exchange traded funds ("ETFs"), since the universe of available alternatives tends to be more expansive than it is for individual stocks. (Even though Ford and GM are both auto manufacturers, their unique, company-specific risks can lead to significant performance differentials over time.) Tax-loss harvesting is a strategy that can prove especially valuable for younger investors or those who do not plan on drawing from their portfolio for a number of years. That's because there's no limit on the amount of losses nor the amount of time those losses can be carried forward. You can capitalize on each market pullback to simultaneously accumulate assets and tax losses, but not actually apply them until years later when drawing down assets from the portfolio.

Punching out from the hazard to the fairway: Occasionally the best offense is a good defense. Upon finding yourself in a difficult spot on the course, it can sometimes make sense to just take your medicine, punch out, and set yourself up for the next shot. It's not always the most exciting play, nor the most fun. But by improving your positioning, you provide yourself with the best opportunity to score well on the hole and for the round overall.

In the midst of a market pullback, we also find ourselves in a less-than-ideal position as the value of our accounts continue to decline. If the market drop is significant enough, punching out of an IRA into a Roth may provide a tremendous setup for your retirement approach. Here's why:

When you contribute to traditional (pre-tax) IRAs, you receive a tax deduction in the year the contribution was made (i.e., $1,000 is contributed to an IRA and reduces the income you earned that year by $1,000). And while the tax deduction is great, you'll have to pay taxes to the IRS when you withdraw assets from the account (and penalties if doing so before 59 1/2).

Conversely, you don't get a tax deduction on your contribution to a Roth IRA, but taxes are also never assessed on those balances again. So, if you contributed $1,000 and the account balance subsequently grew to $1 million, you would have saved taxes on $999,000. Pretty powerful stuff! But how does this translate into an opportunity during a market pullback?

Let's say you have $100,000 within your IRA. You've received your tax deduction and are just riding the wave of tax-deferred growth until you ultimately decide to begin taking money from the account. Along the way, a lending crisis pops up, the economy stalls, and the stock market falls by 50%, dropping your balance to $50,000. Knowing that the market will eventually recover, you take the opportunity to convert[xxiv] the IRA balance into a Roth IRA. While taxes would be due in full on the $50,000 balance that was converted, that amount is now completely tax free to you from now into perpetuity: When the market subsequently recovers, all of the realized growth will never be taxed again. Considering that the market is up nearly 400% (at the time of this writing) since it bottomed in March of 2009, investors who capitalized on this strategy likely benefited tremendously.

Again, it should be noted that taxes would be assessed in the year any balances are converted. Caution should be given to projected taxes to ensure much of the benefit is not wiped out by way of being forced into a higher bracket. But when executed correctly, a punch-out conversion can turn adversity into a tremendous opportunity.

Understanding the nuances of market volatility and when/what particular strategy will provide the most value can be challenging. Fortunately, you don't have to navigate the course alone and can get some help from an advisor along the way. If you choose to partner with an advisor, ensure you receive value from the relationship and that the advisor truly has your best interests at heart. Perhaps the only thing worse than making a catastrophic mistake in managing your finances is making the mistake based on advice you received from someone you were paying to help you!

Hole #8: Need a Caddie? Things to Consider in Partnering with an Advisor

"Nobody but you and your caddie care what you do out there, and if your caddie is betting against you, he doesn't care, either."—Lee Trevino

As an avid golf fan, I tend to watch a fair amount of golf on TV in addition to the rounds I play—even attending a few tournaments to watch in person. Beyond skill set, there is one major difference that I notice between tour players and amateurs: caddies. Of all the golf I have ever seen played professionally, I have yet to see a player who did not have a trusted caddie on his or her bag.

Knowing that the caddie is entitled to a percentage of the winnings if the player finishes in the money, a player entrusts far greater responsibility to the caddie than merely carrying golf clubs. A good caddie knows a course inside and out. They know the location of any particular hole's bailout spots, and which greens aren't going to have as much break as may be thought from reading the terrain alone. A good caddie also keeps their player in the game mentally and on an even keel. In order for a player to decide to enlist the services of a particular caddie, they must feel that those services provide value. The player must find that their ability to score improves by having the caddie at their side.

Otherwise, the caddie is just an added expense, at best.

In much the same way, this model resembles that of an investor deciding whether or not to partner with an advisor. While good advisors can add tremendous value, bad ones can add fees, detract from long-term performance, and deliver advice that may provide more personal benefit to them than you, their client.

While there is no test that can determine with certainty whether an advisor will add or subtract from the number of years you'll spend working prior to reaching your financial goals, by considering the following factors, you can at least improve your odds of finding one capable of saving you a few strokes.

1. **Fiduciary advisor or retail broker:** Imagine going to get fitted for a new set of clubs and learning that the golf pro doing the fitting earns a varying amount of commission dependent upon the brand of clubs you select. That is, he is paid 10% of the club cost if you purchase Brand A, but only 2.5% if you decide to purchase Brand B. Worse yet, the commission schedule changes from month to month, depending on inventory, and each brand's percentage payout varies based on the type of club you are being fitted for (i.e.,

driver, fairway wood, irons, or putter). Confused yet? Welcome to the world of retail brokerage houses.

Retail brokers are commissioned agents of an investment firm who are compensated to sell products to customers. In essence, their primary job is to make money for their company, not necessarily to provide you with the best advice.

Now, does that make all stockbrokers bad people? Absolutely not! I personally and professionally know many brokers who are great family people and citizens of their communities. But even the best among them have an allegiance and duty to maximize profits for their company and its shareholders. If you're trying to minimize the potential opportunities to receive bad advice, be taken advantage of, and eliminate conflicts of interest, you need to be careful. Electing to partner with an individual who is compensated on some metric other than doing right by you may not be the most prudent direction to go.

There is a separate subset of advisor professionals that voluntarily hold themselves to a legal standard which requires that, at all times, they put *your* interests ahead of their own or those of the firm and serve you in what's known as a fiduciary capacity. In the industry, this subset exists in what is known as the Registered Investment Advisor ("RIA") space. The individuals that elect to work in the realm of RIAs are legally obligated by the 1940 Investment Advisors Act to provide guidance to you that he or she feels is in your *best* interest. This legal requirement highlights the key distinction between the two subsets of advisors.

Advisors in the RIA space are bound by law to a fiduciary standard for their clients which requires that they act, at all times, in your best interest. By contrast, retail brokers are bound only by a suitability standard, which requires that they merely confirm the product they are selling be generally *suitable* for your situation.

This somewhat subtle yet extremely significant difference between *best interest* and *suitable for your situation* allows for the introduction of numerous conflicts of interest associated with the advice you might receive. While there may be any number of products that are generally suitable for you (some charging higher fees and paying larger commissions), there are far fewer that would be considered to be in your best interest. The fiduciary is legally obligated to recommend those that are best for you, whereas the broker may be inclined to recommend the one that pays them the most.

Once, you've decided that you'd prefer to partner with a fiduciary advisor (good choice!), how do you know that the person sitting across the table from you actually *is* one? Ask the following questions:

1. **Are you registered with the SEC or FINRA?** FINRA is the governing body for brokers, whereas independent advisors are held accountable to the SEC.
2. **How are you compensated? How are your fees collected?** Independent advisors collect a management fee for the advice they are providing, typically based on the amount of assets over which they are providing guidance. Brokers may or may not charge this management fee but will also collect commissions for investments that are held in your portfolio. Another tip is to look at the advisor/company's website. If you see anywhere on the page "Securities offered through..." that is a good indication the advisor is working for a brokerage house. Independent advisors will custody your

assets with an independent agent such as Fidelity, TD Ameritrade, or Charles Schwab, where they are able to manage your portfolio using many different types of investments (iShares, Vanguard, Dimensional Fund Advisors, etc.) as opposed to those offered only by one company alone.

3. **Do you have a Series 7 license?** A series 7 license is legally required by FINRA in order for brokers to sell securities. It is not required (nor permitted) for independent advisors to have a series 7, since they are not selling you any products. That is, they are not permitted to receive commissions specifically based upon the investments they recommend you purchase. Therefore, holding a series 7 is an indicator that you are speaking with a broker.

4. **Are you serving me as a fiduciary *at all times* and will you put it in writing?** I wish it were as simple as full-time fiduciaries vs. full-time brokers, but unfortunately, there is also a hybrid model that permits an individual to serve in both capacities. Worse yet, such individuals are not required to tell you when they are changing hats from your broker to advisor or back again. You could start a conversation with an advisor outlining a plan that puts your best interests first, but pivot in the middle to a conversation in which he

may be eyeing a commission and never has to tell you!

5. **Will you use an independent custodian or hold my assets in-house?** Like the mere mention of the term "quadruple bogey," hearing the name Bernie Madoff's can instantly trigger feelings of disgust. And, just as there are prudent steps that can be taken to avoid the quadruple bogey, there are steps that can be taken to help avoid being taken advantage of by a scammer like Bernie. One of the most critical is to understand where your assets, those being managed by the advisor, will be held. Think of a custodian as the party that actually holds your money and the advisor as the party that is able to direct which investments to buy and sell with that money. Bernie Madoff was able to scam his investors largely because he was acting as both the advisor and the custodian. He not only was making decisions related to which investments should be bought and sold, he also was the party who had physical possession of all the money. As a result of serving in both capacities, there was no independent means for clients to verify that the assets which Bernie claimed were in his client's accounts actually were in those accounts.

Independent advisors, as mentioned earlier, will work with independent custodians like Fidelity, TD Ameritrade, or Charles Schwab (among others) to provide an additional layer of protection to you. Because you receive information about the value of your accounts from two unrelated entities, it provides an additional opportunity to verify that neither party is treating *your* money as *their* money. That is, the advisor is presenting information that indicates the amount of money they are managing for you, while your custodian is detailing the amount of money actually available in your account. When the custodian and the advisor are one in the same, not only does it become easier to manipulate performance figures being presented to you, but it also becomes much easier for the advisor to embezzle your funds for personal use!

Whenever possible, use a reputable custodian such as the three examples referenced above. Be extremely wary any time you are requested to make a deposit or write a check payable to anyone other than the custodian for your benefit. With the exception of, in very limited cases, payment of fees, an advisor should never have the direct ability to control where your funds are deposited. Taking physical custody of your assets not only increases the probability of being taken advantage of, it is in direct violation of the rules imposed by many of the governing and credentialing bodies in the industry.

6. **What's your education and expertise?** Malcom Gladwell made famous in his book *Outliers* the notion that 10,000 hours of deliberate practice is required to truly master a particular field. He demonstrated how this rule transcends fields from athletics, to computer programming, to medical training, and many others. If you are going to partner with an individual who you are entrusting to provide you with advice related to succeeding with your finances—a major undertaking—it goes without saying this individual should be competent in their field.

Unlike doctors, lawyers, and professional golfers, there aren't many requirements to complete prior to being able to hold oneself out as an advisor. Because of this, credentials and specialization can prove extremely helpful in identifying those that may prove most valuable to you. However, perhaps because there is not a specific track that advisors must take to become qualified to practice, there is also an alphabet soup of designations and mingled letters that advisors can add to the end of their name—181, in fact[xxv]—most of which are not worth the paper they are printed on. That said, some of the more rigorous designations to obtain and, accordingly, some to look for in helping narrow the field of candidates for you, include[xxvi]:

- Chartered Financial Analyst ("CFA")
- Certified Financial Planner ("CFP")
- Certified Public Accountant ("CPA")

While there is no guarantee that merely having any or all of the above credentials will assure you are partnered with a great advisor, the educational and time commitments required by each of the organization's respective governing bodies helps to at least provide assurance that such individuals have a commitment to their profession.

Upon deciding to partner with an advisor, as you proceed through your interview process, make sure you have someone who is competent enough to serve your needs, is someone you feel comfortable with, and is someone that aligns with you philosophically. The process of hiring an advisor should be thought of as a long-term partnership. By having a good understanding of one another's goals, objectives, and financial beliefs at the outset, you can help improve the probability of staying committed to your plan through good times and bad.

Hole #9: Be Prepared for the Joys of the Clubhouse

"One of the most fascinating things about golf is how it reflects the cycle of life. No matter what you shoot, the next day you have to go back to the first tee and begin all over again and make yourself into something."—Peter Jacobson

Not too long ago, I had a great conversation with a friend and fellow dad in regard to a strategy he was using to introduce his son to the great game of golf. Golf's continual challenges and complexity are part of what keeps the game so interesting and engaging but can also be a daunting challenge to overcome when first getting started. I believe this has much to do with the reason many people quit the game shortly after beginning, and even what prevents some from trying to take up the game in the first place. And so, as I spoke with my friend, I was curious to learn more about the strategy he was using to keep his son interested in continuing to play and improve.

In summary it worked like this: For each hole, dad added two strokes to par for his son and then they would play match play games against one another. Basically, a par 4 for dad was a par 6 for son, and whoever had the lowest score relative to *their* par would win the hole. The goal was ultimately to use this same strategy over time, eventually reducing the number of strokes added to par for his son's score as he improved—or started beating dad more consistently. Essentially a handicapping-type strategy, I thought it provided a great way to keep the game competitive and, in turn, keep his son engaged in continuing to learn.

With that in mind, as you've read the pages of this book and begin to outline the shape of your financial plan or start thinking about a transition to retirement, I'd like for you to consider a question: What is your goal? Why are you saving? Aside from aspiring to reach a point at which you feel your assets will provide sufficient income that will no longer *require* you to work, what specifically are you aspiring towards? Have you ever stopped to think about what you will do when you get to that point in life? What will you *do*?

Many a time I've sat with individuals and couples who spend more time planning a two-week vacation than they dedicate to planning their financial goals or how their working years will translate into a fulfilling retirement lifestyle. The result typically isn't positive: overspending to cope with feeling a lack of value...regretting the decision to leave a longtime employer while having no opportunity to be rehired...the selling of a business that took years to build and was the source of tremendous pride, translating post-sale into a lost sense of self.

Far too often we sell ourselves short in not only planning for how we will reach our financial goals, but also by failing to plan what success actually looks like once we get there. A better understanding of what success looks like will make saving easier as you're able to picture why you are saving—rather than merely throwing money into a savings bucket. It will also help you maintain a sense of purpose and fulfillment upon reaching your goals. From my experience in helping hundreds of individuals navigate this same journey, I've found the below exercises most helpful in achieving a positive transition from success to significance.

1. **Visualize:** Anyone who has watched Jason Day play a round of golf knows his pre-shot routine begins with an intense focus of picturing the exact shot he is getting ready to hit. What will it feel like? What flight path will the ball follow? Where will it land? Having a vivid picture of the exact outcome he is trying to achieve enables his mind to tell his body what it needs to do. As alluded to earlier in this book, the benefits of visualization have been shown to improve a saver's ability to increase their deferrals when envisioning an older version of themselves. It's also a way to stay better committed to a plan over an extended period of time and a great way to refine your

financial goals. For example, what would a typical day look like for you if you were financially independent? What would you do? Where would you live? How will you interact socially? How will you continue to stimulate your mind? While you don't necessarily need to have every hour of every day planned out, by having an understanding of these questions, you can start to gain better clarity over what is required to achieve your goals and when you may expect to achieve them. With this understanding, you can begin building a plan to get there.

2. **Review and Update:** The strategy my friend used to get his son interested in the game of golf was one that he can review and tailor over time as circumstances change, helping ensure the overall *intent* of his strategy— introducing his son to the game of golf— stays timely and relevant. Similarly, you must periodically evaluate whether your strategy remains appropriate. Do you still enjoy doing the things you do today that you did five years ago? Will changes in health impact any of your planned activities? For better or worse, things change over time. As they do, it's important to make sure your plan stays current as a means to keep your

vision fresh, maintain focus, and ensure your strategy remains consistent with your goals.

3. **Practice:** As you near financial independence, if at all possible, it can be a great idea to practice what that life may look like. For business owners, this may mean phasing out your time in the office as others are able to take over your day-to-day responsibilities. For others, it may mean simply taking a long stay-cation, whereby you take an extended period off of work but plan to stay at home rather than travel. Using practice activities like this can provide perspective on whether your plan is appropriate for you after all. If you find yourself bored within the first two weeks of your practice period, perhaps it would be a good idea to reconsider your strategy and prevent feelings of regret before it's too late. Just like golf, the more relevant you can make your practice sessions to the real thing, the better prepared you'll be when encountering the situations and the stakes are higher.

I am forever indebted to the game of golf for the opportunities it continues to provide me to spend time with my own family and friends. The thought of having a game I can play my entire life, in the company of best friends and family, is a gift no amount of money could purchase. However, with the exception of a select few who are fortunate enough to be able to call the game a profession, most of us will need to continue to plan and strategize so that one day we will not have to call off work to enjoy a quick 9 holes or a leisurely 18. My hope is that by following the tips and strategies outlined in this book, you'll be well on your way much sooner than later.

So, cheers to only low numbers on your scorecard and ever-growing ones on your financial statement!

About the Author

Kyle carries a 10 handicap, is a husband, father of three, CFA Charterholder, and Certified Financial Planner® planning professional with a strong passion for golf and helping individuals achieve their financial goals.

With a professional background that ranges from helping clients determine the value of their privately held businesses to assisting them with prioritizing their spending and savings goals, Kyle has 10+ years of experience assisting clients in navigating their unique course to financial prosperity. He has deep expertise in the areas of investment management, estate planning, and in-depth financial planning. He is a firm believer in the fiduciary service model, which prioritizes client needs at all times and seeks to eliminate as many conflicts of interest as possible from the client–advisor relationship.

As the product of two great parents who dedicated their lives to public education, Kyle has experienced firsthand the positive impact education can have in creating opportunity and improving outcomes. He believes that by working to increase financial literacy, individuals will be less likely to fall for predatory schemes that so often prove catastrophic to their plans. By better understanding their finances, individuals will be more empowered to live their lives without worrying how to finance them.

Endnotes

---

[i] This example assumes a growth rate of 8% per year throughout the entire time period.

[ii] Dushi, Irena & Honig, Marjorie. "How Much Do Respondents in the Health and Retirement Study Know About Their Tax-deferred Contribution Plans? A Crosscohort Comparison." December 2008. (https://deepblue.lib.umich.edu/bitstream/handle/2027.42/64473/wp201.pdf;jsessionid=AF553DD41F5A346EEF13453459D35B82?sequence=1))

[iii] Sims, T., Bailenson, J., & Carstensen, L.L. (2015). Connecting to Your Future Self: Enhancing Financial Planning among Diverse Communities Using Virtual Technology. (http://vhil.stanford.edu/pubs/2015/connecting-to-your-future-self/)

[iv] As of 12/31/2016 based on research completed by the Investment Company Institute.

[v] Riepe, Mark. "Does Market Timing Work?" Schwab Center for Financial Research, 2013. Returns based on the S&P 500 over the period 1993 - 2012.

[vi] Yardini Research Inc. "Market Briefing: S&P 500 Bull & Bear Markets & Corrections" July 2, 2018.

[vii] The Morningstar Mirage - https://www.wsj.com/articles/the-morningstar-mirage-1508946687?mg=prod/accounts-wsj

[viii] MSCI EAFE

[ix] NAREIT Equity Index

[x] MSCI EME

[xi] As measured by the Barclays Aggregate Bond Index.

[xii] While each individual's circumstances will vary, typically it is advisable to hold between 3-6 months' living expenses in a liquid savings account.

[xiii] Roger G. Ibbotson and Paul D. Kaplan. *Does Asset Allocation Policy Explain 40, 90, or 100 Percent of Performance?* Financial Analysts Journal January/February 2010.

[xiv] James X. Xiong, CFA, Roger G. Ibbotson, Thomas M. Idzorek, CFA, and Peng Chen, CFA. The Equal Importance of Asset Allocation and Active Management. Financial Analysts Journal 2010 Volume 66. https://www.cfapubs.org/doi/pdf/10.2469/faj.v66.n2.7

[xv] Q1 2018 Guide to the Markets. JP Morgan Asset Management.

[xvi] Remember that past performance never guarantees future results!

[xvii] As of 10/30/2017. FB contributed 4.6% of the S&P's total return, AMZN contributed 4.2%, and Alphabet Class A & C contributed 2.2% and 2.3%, respectively.

[xviii] Market capitalization is a term commonly used to assess the size of publicly traded companies. It is simply a calculation that multiples a company's stock price by the number of shares outstanding.

[xix] As measured by Market Capitalization based on 2016 data from: https://data.worldbank.org

[xx] https://www.firstquadrant.com/system/files/0003_How_Well_Have_Taxable_Investors_Been_Served_0.pdf

[xxi] http://www.icifactbook.org/fb_ch5.html

[xxii] Which is highly illegal to trade upon—FYI!

[xxiii] Assumes a $100,000 investment in the S&P 500 from October 2007–October 2017.

[xxiv] Conversions should not be confused with withdrawals/distributions. To avoid significant tax complications, conversions should go directly from the IRA to the Roth IRA without you ever taking physical possession of the assets.

[xxv] At the time of this writing, FINRA referenced 181 professional, industry designations on its website.

[xxvi] For additional details on these designations, I would encourage a review of the website: https://www.investopedia.com/articles/professionaleducation/08/cfa-cpa-cfp-how-to-choose.asp

www.ingramcontent.com/pod-product-compliance
Lightning Source LLC
Chambersburg PA
CBHW022059210326
41520CB00046B/716